101 Creative Ideas
for Animal-Assisted Therapy

101 Creative Ideas
for Animal-Assisted Therapy

**Interventions for AAT Teams and
Working Professionals**

Stacy Grover

Published in the United States of America by:
Published in the USA by:

www.MotivationalPress.com

Printed in the United States of America

ISBN   13: 978-0-9825755-8-1

Book and cover design by Darlene Swanson • www.van-garde.com

Proceeds from the sale of this book will go to Therapy Animals of Utah, a nonprofit organization.

The methods described in this book are intended for those who have already received training in Animal-Assisted Therapy. Individual animals may respond differently to the activities described in this book. Caution must be employed when working with animals to avoid transmission of disease and the possibility of injury. The author of this work is not responsible for injury or illness resulting from application of the methods described in this work.

Acknowledgements

This book wouldn't be possible without Debbie Carr, who contributed to the activities, contacted professionals, and let me run ideas past her at all hours; Judy Peter, Vanessa Rapier, OTR, and Lenore Davis, MS, SLP, CCC, who added their expertise and their great ideas related to their respective fields; the good-looking clients and teams who let me follow them around with a camera and use their pictures, the members of TAU, who with their animals give so much of their time to visit others, Nancy Walton, who mentored us and has the biggest heart of anyone I know; Gary Walton, who kept me enthused about the project and made this book possible, Cosita and Liberty, who seem almost magical in their ability to connect with people, and especially the many amazing people in all the places we've visited who share their lives and love with us.

#4 Sitting In a Garden . . . Scooby sits with a client.

Contents

The Purpose of
This Resource

Perhaps you're a human service professional who believes in
the power of the human/animal bond. You'd like to use Animal-
Assisted Therapy (AAT) to help your clients meet their goals.
You've been trained in how to implement AAT into your program
and have arranged for a trained animal/handler team to visit your
facility on a regular basis.

Maybe you're a volunteer who has been trained in Animal-
Assisted Therapy. Your animal partner has proven that she/he
has the skills and aptitude to enjoy this work. You've assessed
the facility where you're going, met the professional with whom
you're working, and gathered your supplies.

Now What?

That's where this book can help. It is a collection of ideas for
utilizing AAT, though it is by no means a comprehensive list.
You will find as you gain experience you will think of your own
activities to add to these, as there is no limit to where your

imagination will take you! There is space at the end of each section for you to add your own notes and ideas, or you may log onto www.aatideas.com to read others' ideas and add your own. They just might be used in the next edition of this book!

This booklet is not intended to be a course in Animal-Assisted Therapy. If you're looking for such training, consult the resources in the appendix at the back of this book.

Who Is Involved in These Interventions?

1. A working professional: The professional could be a teacher or a therapist. Her job is to select appropriate clients and choose appropriate goals. The professional works with the handler and client to determine which intervention to use. Then she teaches or provides therapy throughout. The professional is primarily responsible for the well-being of the client.

2. A handler: The handler must be an expert at reading his animal's signals. He needs to work with the professional in choosing interventions that are appropriate for his animal. The handler interacts with the professional, client, and animal partner during the intervention. He maintains control of the animal partner at all times, and advocates for the safety and comfort of the animal. He is primarily responsible for the well-being of the animal.

3. An animal partner: Many different animals are very successful in AAT. This book specifically addresses working with dogs, cats, small animals, birds, and horses.[1] The animal partner must

---

1. While hippotherapy and therapeutic riding are very effective branches of animal-assisted therapy, this book does not address this aspect of AAT.

have a strong bond with the handler, enjoy meeting new people and visiting new places. He must be healthy, skilled in basic obedience, and under control at all times. He should be evaluated and registered with a well-known Animal-Assisted Therapy Organization. The animal partner is responsible for connecting with the client.

4. A client: The client can be of any age. He needs to enjoy animals and not be allergic to them. He must not have any communicable diseases or open wounds that cannot be covered. He needs to have enough motor/behavioral control to interact safely with the animal.

5: Facility and staff: Before beginning an AAT program, the facility needs to be assessed as a safe place for animals and the administration must be supportive. Particular care should be taken to understand and follow though with all of the facility's policies and procedures, especially those regarding infection control. For a sample set of policies and procedures, contact the Delta Society.

Choosing the Right Interventions

The therapist, handler, and sometimes the client need to meet to choose interventions. The following factors must be considered in order to ensure the effectiveness as well as the comfort and safety of all involved.

1. The intervention needs to match the client. The client and therapist need to give serious thought to selecting an intervention that matches the client. Not all interventions are appropriate for everyone.

2. The intervention needs to match the animal. The animal's size, temperament, experience, and skills need to be considered when choosing an activity for him to do. For example, a small dog will feel much more comfortable sitting on a lap than walking on the floor through a crowded hallway. The handler should decide which interventions match her animal.

3. The intervention needs to match the client's goal. Animal-Assisted Therapy fits into almost any existing treatment/ educational plan. It just takes a little imagination and creativity to add the motivating factor of an animal.

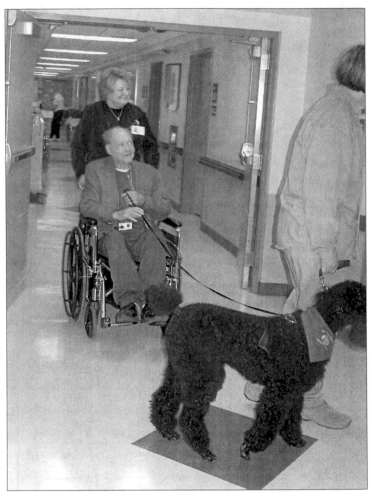

#33 Going Visiting . . . A client takes Liberty around
the facility, sharing her with other residents.

Tweaking Interventions

Most of the interventions in this book can be adapted to fit many different goals just by changing the circumstances a bit. The following is an example of this.

Let's look at activity #2, Grooming.

Grooming: The handler has in their gearbag the animal's grooming supplies. Use these supplies to groom the animal. Rhythmic brushing can be very relaxing and therapeutic for the client as well as the animal partner. The client could brush the animal's teeth and clean nails or hooves. Some handlers even paint their dog's toenails. If you choose to do this, I would recommend using a children's nail polish that doesn't have a strong scent and washes or peels off easily. Extension: After grooming the animal, have your clients wash their hands and groom themselves--brushing their hair, teeth, etc.

At first glance, this activity seems to address only grooming skills, but let's tweak it a bit.

❧ If the animal partner is placed on the left side of the client, and the client brushes with the right hand, grooming now addresses the goal of crossing midline.

❧ Have the client stand while brushing. Focus on posture and balance.

❧ Discuss brushing gently on the animal's back, with the goal of learning appropriate touch.

❧ Have the client hold and release a brush or use a squirt bottle, learning grasping and releasing skills.

❧ Count the number of brush strokes; grooming then becomes an exercise in counting.

❧ Have the client choose friends with whom to groom the animal partner to address social skills.

❧ Discuss the responsibilities of caring for a pet while grooming, addressing the goal of accepting responsibility.

❧ Painting the animal's nails, and opening various containers addresses fine motor skills.

- ❧ Offer praise to the client, and have the client praise the animal partner for how good he/she looks. Grooming then addresses the goal of accepting and receiving praise.

- ❧ Give the client a choice of brushes, or locations to groom, and you've addressed the goal of decision-making and empowerment.

- ❧ Discuss groomers, and grooming becomes an exercise in career education.

- ❧ For a student who is learning English or needs to increase his/her vocabulary, teach the English vocabulary for brush, spray, comb, etc. before grooming.

- ❧ Have the client match her breathing with the brush strokes. Then the exercise works on breath support.

- ❧ For the speech goal of being able to say /ch/ in isolation, have the client repeat ch, ch, ch when spraying leave-in conditioner.

It only takes a little creativity to tweak interventions to meet your goals!

Interventions

When looking at the following interventions, you will see these symbols designed to help you determine which intervention best matches each type of animal.

Cat	Dog	Small Animal	Bird	Horse

Each intervention has a corresponding number. The purpose of the numbers is to make finding a particular intervention more accessible.

Remember to have all involved wash their hands before and after every activity/intervention. See activity #62.

Bonding Moments

These interventions include activities that require just one client and one animal. Of course the handler and professional are also involved. They are designed to encourage the human/animal bond.

1. **Nurturing:** Often residents of a skilled-nursing facility have spent their entire lives nurturing others, only to find that now they are the ones being nurtured. Children, who are most often cared for, also appreciate the opportunity to be on the giving end. Here the client has the opportunity to take care of the animal partner, including activities such as feeding, providing water, getting the animal partner to sleep, or taking him out to relieve himself.

2. **Grooming:** The handler has in the gearbag the animal's grooming supplies. Use these supplies to groom the animal. Rhythmic brushing can be very relaxing and therapeutic for the client as well as the animal partner. The client could brush the animal partner's teeth and clean nails or hooves. Some handlers

even paint their dog's toenails. If you choose to do this, I would recommend using a children's nail polish that doesn't have a strong scent and washes or peels off easily. Extension: After grooming the animal partner, have your clients wash their hands and groom themselves-- brushing their hair, teeth, etc.

3.   **Up Close and Personal:** This is an opportunity for the client and animal partner to spend high-quality, uninterrupted time together. This can occur on a bed, a couch, using the bedside table, standing, or sitting on the floor. The animal partner gets up close and personal with the client. The client has the opportunity to express and receive affection and acceptance, smell the animal's freshly groomed scent, feel its body heat, snuggle with, pet and talk with the animal partner.

4.   **Sitting In A Garden:** Often just the presence of an animal is therapeutic. In this activity the animal partner simply spends time with the client while the client sits in the garden and enjoys being outside.

5.   **Offering Treats:** The handler brings treats for the client to offer to the animal.

The client follows directions to offer the treats in a safe manner. See Appendix B for treat recipes.

6. **Petting:** Rhythmic Petting can be very relaxing to both the animal partner and the client. The animal and client can be positioned in many different ways to meet the client's goals. Some positions could include sitting, standing, standing on uneven surfaces, placing the animal partner up high, down low, in front of, on the left or right side of the client.

7. **Eyes On Me:** Have the client make and maintain eye contact with the animal partner by holding a treat at the tip of her own nose for 10 seconds and asking the animal partner to watch. At the end of the 10 seconds, the client gives the animal partner the treat

Add your own ideas for bonding moments in this space!

Time To Play

Playing is an important aspect of life, not just for children, but for adults too! Therapy animals enjoy playing with us, so forget your troubles and come laugh and play!

8. **Animal Bingo:** With the participants, make a list of 25 words that either remind them of the animal partner, or apply to the goal/intervention of the day. Have them put one word in each square of a Bingo sheet. Then play Bingo with the list, while the animal partner spends time with the clients. Extension: Give the clients ready-made Bingo sheets, or pictures instead of words in the spaces.

9. **Blowing Bubbles:** Chicken or beef-flavored bubbles can be purchased from animal supply catalogs. In this activity, the client blows bubbles while the dog runs around and tries to catch them. I suggest that the handler try this at home first to learn if the dog is interested.

10. **Dance Party:** Provide animal-themed music and have a dance with the therapy animal. Provide

human treats and dog treats. See Appendix A for animal-themed music, and Appendix B for animal treat recipes.

11.   **Dog-Dog-Cat:** This game is played like Duck, Duck, Goose. Participants sit in a circle. The handler sits in the middle, with the animal partner on leash, being petted by the children in the circle. One person is chosen to be the cat. Walking around the circle, she stops at each person and says "cat." When the cat reaches her chosen person, she says "dog," instead of cat. The chosen "dog" jumps up and chases the "cat" around the circle. If the cat runs around the circle and sits back in the empty space before the dog catches him, the dog becomes the cat and starts the game again. If the dog tags the cat before they sit down, the cat sits in the middle of the circle with the handler and animal partner until the next person is tagged and comes to the center.

12.   **Fetch:** A dog who enjoys retrieving will enjoy this intervention. The clients throw the ball, the dog retrieves it, and the participants take turns throwing again. The clients can be sitting or standing. Extensions: Instead of a ball throw a stuffed toy or Frisbee. The client could use a ball launcher, roll the ball, kick the ball, throw one handed or two handed, overhand or underhand. The

professional could also throw the ball to the client to catch before the client throws it for the dog.

13. **Fido Says:** This game is played like Simon Says, except the name of the animal partner is substituted for Simon. The handler calls out actions that the animal partner can do. For example, the handler and animal partner stand at the front and say, "Fido says bark like a dog." Everyone barks like a dog. Then they say, "Roll over." No one rolls over because Fido didn't say so. If players do the action without Fido saying so, they go to the outside of the group and continue to play. The last person playing in the center is the winner. Examples of actions could be: play dead, shake, speak, run, walk, lay down, etc.

14. **Grab Bag:** After going over the items the handler brought in the gear bag, have the client reach a hand into the bag without looking. Name an object inside, and ask him to feel around and find it.

15. **Follow the Leader:** Have students take turns being the leader. Everyone else lines up behind the leader and follows, including the handler and therapy dog, walking in the same manner as the leader. Take turns being the leader.

16.   **Hide and Seek:** A dog who is toy-motivated or a good tracker will enjoy this game and so will the clients. The handler or one participant blocks the dog's view while another participant hides the dog's favorite toy somewhere in the area. They then watch the dog search the room trying to find the toy. Discussion is encouraged. Extension: Have a client hide with a treat. The dog then needs to come find the client to get the treat.

17.   **Memory:** Use the objects in the handler's gear bag to play a visual memory game. Have the clients observe the objects for a set amount of time. Then put the objects back in the bag. Have them write down as many items as they can remember. Another way to play is after they observe the items, have them close their eyes. The handler takes away an item and participants tell what is missing. The clients can be enjoying the therapy animal while playing the game.

18.   **Movie and Popcorn:** Show an animal-themed movie and have the clients spend time up close and personal with the animal partner while watching the movie. Provide popcorn and share with the therapy animal. Extension: Watch home videos of the therapy animal.

19. **Musical Dots:** Count the number of children playing, and scatter that many numbered 6-inch dots on the floor. For example, if there are 10 children, there should be 10 dots on the floor, numbered 1-10. When the music starts (see the appendix for animal-themed music) the children randomly wander around the room. When the music stops, they each stand on a dot. The handler/animal partner calls out a number. Whoever is standing on the dot with the matching number becomes the next leader, and the AAT team takes their place on a dot. This can be adapted to having dots of different colors, dots with math problems or answers to math problems, vocabulary words, speech sounds, etc. on them.

20. **Obstacle Course:** Have the client take the animal partner and handler through an obstacle course. The client could either work alone or as a team. Clients could design the obstacle course themselves. This could also be done as a relay race, or timed.

21. **Off and Take It:** In this activity, the client puts a treat somewhere where the animal partner can reach it, for example on their hand, foot, knee, couch or bed. The dog is given the command "Off." The dog waits until the client says, "Take it!" at which time he can eat the treat.

22.   **Password:** Make cards with words pertaining to the animal partner or the focus of the lesson. For example, if you're working on health and safety that day, words could include: collar, leash, fence, seatbelt, 911, fruit, strangers, address, phone number, veggies, nutrition, hand-washing, flu shots, etc. Put the cards in the animal's vest pocket or gear bag. Have the clients form two teams. The animal partner and handler can sit between the teams so participants on both sides can enjoy time with the animal. Have one client draw a card. Give him a set number of seconds to get his team to guess the word by giving verbal clues. If the team guesses the word they get a point and the next team takes a turn. Extensions: Instead of verbal clues for the word, have the player draw, sculpt with clay, act it out, or cut it out. Or have the player roll a die: 1 means verbal clues, 2 means drawing clues, 3 means sculpting clues, 4 means acting clues, 5 means cutting clues, and 6 is player's choice.

23.   **Red Light Green Light:** This game is played like Red Light Green Light except the green light is a "bark" from the therapy dog. This game works well for dogs who know the speak command. Students line up on one side of the gym. The handler and dog, along with one player, the traffic controller, stands at the other side

of the gym facing them. The handler asks the animal partner to speak. When the dog barks, everyone runs toward the traffic controller. When the traffic controller calls out "Red Light!" everyone freezes. If the controller spots anyone moving, that person has to go back to the wall and start again. The dog keeps barking and the child keeps saying "Red Light!" until someone crosses the gym and tags the wall. This child then becomes the next traffic controller and stands with the handler and dog. Extension: Have the handler and animal partner join the crowd crossing the room. This works well for an animal partner who knows the "wait" command.

24. **Soccer:** Some dogs enjoy pushing around a big ball with their nose. In this game, the client kicks the ball and the dog goes to get it. They can pass the ball back and forth between them.

25. **Teaching Tricks:** This activity works with an animal partner who knows tricks. (*See the Resources section at the back of the book.*) The handler teaches the client how to do tricks with the animal partner using either a clicker or treats as positive reinforcement. This can be done with the client alone or with a friend. Extensions: The client and team demonstrate the tricks to others. The client could also teach the animal partner

a trick he doesn't know yet. Discuss with the client the importance of positive reinforcement. After the activity, have him practice reinforcing his peers with the positive skills he learned from training the animal.

26.   **The Cup Game:** This game gets people talking with each other and to the dog. First, the professional chooses three or four people to play. They all get a small cup to hold. The handler turns the dog around so she can't see the clients. The professional puts a dog treat in one of the cups. Then the handler leads the dog from person to person, letting her sniff the cups for the treat. After she finds and eats it, the handler turns the dog around and the professional puts a treat in a different cup for the dog to find.

27.   **Treasure Hunt:** Bury smelly dog treats and small plastic animals or other items in a sandbox. You can find inexpensive, plastic toy dogs in the toy section of your local drugstore. Have the dog hunt for treats and the clients hunt for the plastic animals. Extension: The first player to find five items is the winner. You could also set the timer. At the end of one minute see who has found the most items. Have someone count how many treats the animal partner found.

28.   **Treat Hunt:** This game takes place outside in the grass. Each client gets a few pieces of a smelly treat. Have them throw the treats randomly out in the grass. Watch as the dog looks for the treats. Discussion is encouraged.

29.   **What Now?** This is a great activity for choosing an activity to do that day. Have several activities from this book written on cards. Put the cards in the pocket of the animal's vest or gear bag. Have the client draw a card from the vest. Whichever card they draw indicates the activity for the day.

30.   **You Blew It!:** This activity works well with a small dog who is ball-motivated. Have the client blow a Ping-Pong ball across the table. When the ball falls off the other end of the table, the dog scrambles to get it and bring it back. Don't play this game if the dog has a tendency to swallow or crunch small balls. Extensions: Have the client blow the ball across the surface of water instead of a table surface. The client could also blow a downy feather instead of a ball for a cat to chase.

Add your own playful ideas in this space!

Making Friends

Animals are fabulous at instigating social interaction. These activities are designed to encourage clients to interact and communicate with each other. The "Time to Play" activities are also very effective at this.

31.   **Beauty Parlor:** The client chooses a few friends. They set up a beauty parlor and groom the animal partner together. (See item 2, "Grooming," for ideas.)

32.   **Candid Camera:** In this activity, clients have their picture taken with the animal. These can be taken with a facility digital camera or a Polaroid camera. Encourage them to look at each others' pictures and discuss them. Extensions: They can also decorate frames on which to mount the photos. Instead of getting their own picture taken, they can also opt to take a picture of just the animal. The picture can be hung on their bedroom wall. This is a great intervention to help clients who have difficulty remembering the team from week-to-week.

33. **Going Visiting:** The client takes the animal partner and handler for a walk through the facility, introducing the animal partner and sharing her with others. This can be a wheelchair walk if the client uses a wheelchair (see activity 55). Extension: the client and team could prepare a poster advertising to those in the facility when the therapy animal will be coming.

34. **Good Friends:** Have the clients list the reasons they like the animal. Then have them take that list and figure out how they can use the same skills to be a good friend (Ex: He's always excited to spend time with me, he's never too busy, he's a good listener, etc.)

35. **Sit and Share:** The client and team sit in the lobby or common room, where the client introduces the team to others and encourages them to join in talking and petting the animal partner.

36. **Sportsmanship:** Hold a race with all of the participants including the handler and animal. Have the handler and animal partner lose the race. Note the animal's reaction when he loses. Race again. This time the handler and animal partner need to win. Note the

animal's actions when he wins. Discuss how an animal partner is a great example of sportsmanship and really, the fun part for him is running, not winning or losing. He also doesn't get upset with his partner for slowing him down!

37.   **Thanks:** Have the client practice showing appreciation to the animal, handler, and professional who made the visit possible.

Add your own ideas for making friends in this space!

Let's Talk

A therapy animal working with a professional facilitates the discussion of many topics. These interventions are ways to incorporate animals into the discussion.

38. **Chores:** Discuss the work involved in having an animal, such as feeding, watering, spending time with them, cleaning up, going to the vet, etc. Extension: Act the chores out with the animal partner. Students could also discuss household/classroom/facility chores; who's responsible for them and how it impacts the group if someone doesn't do their job.

39. **Commonalities:** This is a very powerful metaphoric tool in the hands of skilled therapists. Using carefully selected children's literature or actual or contrived stories about the animal, discuss feelings or situations that apply to the client's goals. Have the client identify times when she's felt the same as the animal in the story. Then discuss helpful ways for the animal and the client to deal with those feelings. For example, if the client is dealing with abandonment issues,

discuss the story of when the animal left its mother to
live with the handler. Let the client describe how the
animal partner felt and connect it to her own feelings and
situation. The therapist can then discuss with the client
her own feelings of abandonment. Extension: The client
could also observe the animal's body language and apply
them to human feelings and responses. An example of this
might be the client saying, "The dog's head is on her paws.
She's probably sick and tired of being here and wants to go
home to her own house." The therapist can then discuss
with the client her own feelings of wanting to go home.

40.   **Gear Bag:** The handler
pulls out items from the gear bag one by one, and before
they are explained, allows the client to guess how the
animal partner and handler use each item.

41.   **Photo Album:** The handler
brings a photo album of the animal: where she lives,
what her family is like, what she likes doing, her puppy
pictures, etc. While the animal partner is snuggled up
with the client, the client can be discussing, looking at,
and reading the album with the professional and handler.

42.   **Reminiscing:** Reminiscing
about animals can be done one-on-one, or with a group.

The animal partner is with the client, being petted and discussed. Extension: Have cards on which are written several "reminiscing" questions, such as "Describe your childhood pet," or "Did you have outside animals or inside animals?" The residents take turns drawing cards, answering questions, and reminiscing.

43. **Staying Safe:** Discuss and show the things the handler does to keep the animal partner safe, i.e.: collar, seatbelt, leash, keeping doors closed, fenced yard, etc. Discuss how horrible it would be if anything happened to the animal. Then talk about personal safety and what steps they need to do to stay safe. (Ex: not talking to strangers; knowing their phone number and address, etc.)

44. **Stressin':** Teach the clients about the calming strategies of the therapy animal, i.e.: yawning, lip licking, turning away, panting, fluffing feathers, pinning ears back, etc. The clients can imitate some of these strategies if they would like. Then discuss human self-calming strategies. Discuss stressors, both animal and human, and think of helpful ways of responding to them.

45.   **Translations:** This activity involves the client learning about animal behavior. The client observes the animal's behavior and then interprets what the animal partner is feeling. Extension: Have the client observe and interpret the animal's reactions to human behavior. For example, "The dog turns his head every time I talk loudly. He must be nervous when I use such a loud voice." The client can also predict the behavior the animal partner would show as a result of a hypothetical situation. This ties in well with predicting how other people will react to the client's behavior.

46.   **Trivia:** Ask the client to recall facts about the animal partner that were learned during a previous visit. See how many facts the client can remember.

47.   **Twenty Questions:** In this activity, the client asks or answers questions about the animal. Extension: List the words Who, What, Where, When, Why, and How for the clients to choose when forming their questions. The clients could also write down their questions before asking them.

Add your own ideas for discussion in this space!

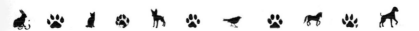

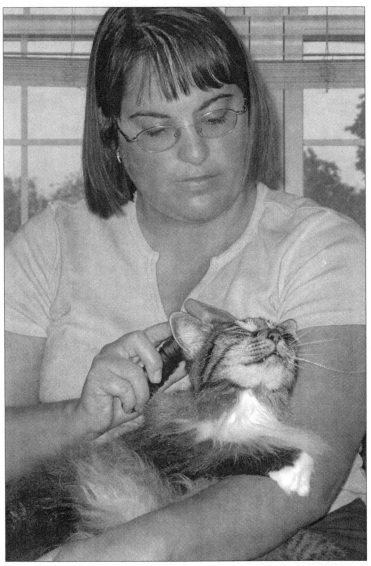

#2 Grooming . . . Jingles relaxes as she's brushed.

Create Something Great

Animals have inspired many artists to create masterpieces. Let your clients find the artist in themselves by creating something great.

48.	**Animal Artists:** Clients can use brushes, clay, pencils, watercolors, or other mediums to create their own masterpieces with the animal partner as the inspiration for their creations.

49.	**Collage Art:** Using pet supply catalogs and animal magazines have the clients cut out pictures that pertain to the discussion of the day and create a collage, gluing the pictures onto paper.

50.	**Making Copies:** Give each artist a line drawing of the animal. Many photo software programs have the ability to change a photo to a line drawing. If you don't have access to such a program, find a line drawing of the breed. Provide them with a piece of tracing paper and have them trace the picture.

51. **Murals:** Have the students draw a picture of the animal. Then draw a square-inch grid over the drawing. Provide large strips of butcher paper for each artist. Have them draw a square-foot grid on it. Then enlarge the drawing into a mural, square-by-square.

52. **Paw Prints:** Using washable paint, have the animal partner make paw/hoof/footprints. Some clients might enjoy trying to draw the paw prints freehand, or making a print of their own hand or foot. Extension: Study fingerprints or research tracking.

53. **Shape Up:** Give each artist a paper with a variety of shapes drawn on it. Have them cut out the shapes, then assemble them in the shape of the therapy animal. This can also be done with tangrams.

54. **Trendy T-shirts:** Using different colors of fabric paint, decorate a t-shirt with an animal theme. You can have the animal partner leave footprints on the shirt, or provide stencils and sponges in animal shapes. Extensions: Make an iron-on of a picture of the therapy animal. Iron them onto the shirts. You could also purchase a plain dog t-shirt and paint him a shirt too!

Add your own artistic ideas in this space!

Caregiving

Many clients we visit have very little opportunity to care for others. One of the great things about companion animals is that they need humans to do things for them. These interventions empower clients by letting them care for the therapy animal.

55. **Going For a Walk:** 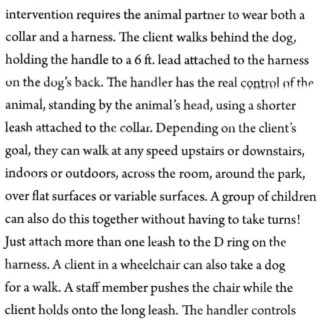 This intervention requires the animal partner to wear both a collar and a harness. The client walks behind the dog, holding the handle to a 6 ft. lead attached to the harness on the dog's back. The handler has the real control of the animal, standing by the animal's head, using a shorter leash attached to the collar. Depending on the client's goal, they can walk at any speed upstairs or downstairs, indoors or outdoors, across the room, around the park, over flat surfaces or variable surfaces. A group of children can also do this together without having to take turns! Just attach more than one leash to the D ring on the harness. A client in a wheelchair can also take a dog for a walk. A staff member pushes the chair while the client holds onto the long leash. The handler controls

the animal partner using the short leash attached to the collar. This can also be adapted to pushing a small animal in a stroller, or in the lap of a client in a wheelchair.

56.   **Preparing For a Walk:** The client puts the equipment on the animal, preparing to go for a walk. This activity is great for fastening buttons, buckles, tying scarves, lifting saddles, etc. Extension: Have the client work on dressing herself after practicing with the animal.

57.   **Selecting Stuff:** In this activity, the handler spreads out the contents of the supply bag she carries. When she needs an item, she asks the client to select it. Depending on the client's goals, adaptations might include selecting items by handing the item to the handler, by eye gaze, using yes/no responses, reaching, pointing, signing, or using a communication board.

58.   **Peanut Butter:** Most dogs love dog biscuits. They like them even more when they have peanut butter or easy cheese spread on them. The clients could spread their own peanut butter or cheese on crackers and have a picnic with the therapy dogs!

59. **Tongue-ersize:** This activity is meant to demonstrate putting the tongue in certain positions. One way is to have the animal partner roll over on her back. The animal's tongue will naturally fall to the back of the mouth, demonstrating the /g/ or /k/ position. Another way to demonstrate tongue movement is to put a little bit of peanut butter or easy cheese on the animal's nose. Therapy animals will do entertaining things with their tongues to get it. Watch what the animal partner does, then have the client try to do the same with his tongue. What great motivation for doing oral-motor exercises!

60. **Yoga:** Yoga is an effective form of exercise and meditation that helps to increase flexibility and well-being. Recently, several yoga instructors have included dogs in their classes. For this intervention, the client participates in yoga with a therapy dog.

61. **Kitchen Time:** This activity works well for an animal partner who is a good eater. Have the clients make homemade treats for the animal. Give some to the animal partner and either keep the rest for the next visit, or send them home with the handler. See Appendix B for recipes.

62. **Hand Washing:** Have the clients wash their hands before and after interacting with the animal. Discuss the importance of hand washing to prevent getting sick and spreading germs.

63. **Tiny Treats:** Before giving the animal partner treats, use scissors to cut them into small pieces. This works very well for soft treats such as pepperoni-type dog treats. Extension: For multiplication/fraction and division practice, figure out how many sticks you'll need to cut in order to have enough for each participant to give the animal partner five treats, or how many treats each participant will have if one stick is cut into 10 treats, and we cut three sticks, etc.

**#67 Lights, Camera, Action . . .
Bayou charms the crowd as
he sits on Santa's finger.**

Add your own caregiving ideas in this space.

Lots to Learn

These activities are designed for students in an educational setting. Some activities are well-suited for small children and others for higher grades. They're divided into subjects.

Language Arts

64. **Authors:** Have the client write a story, poem, play, or song about the animal. They could then illustrate it. They could also act out their story with the animal partner and take pictures or video.

65. **Compare and Contrast:** Compare the therapy animal to people. A graphic organizer such as a Venn Diagram can be used. Extensions: Compare different types of animals, such as big dogs and little dogs, reptiles and mammals, the therapy cat and a cat character in a book, a mother dog and a puppy, etc

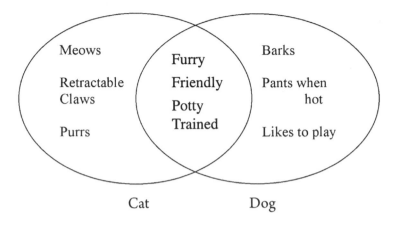

66.   **Fact and Opinion:** Spend some time with the animal. Then, using a t-chart, have the students list facts and opinions about the animal.

Example:

Facts	Opinions
The cat is black.	Cats are better than dogs.
She has a rough tongue.	Cats' tongues are creepy.

67.   **Lights, Camera, Action!** Have the clients put on costumes and act out a story with the animal partner playing a part. The animal partner does not wear a costume, only the human actors get to dress up. Draw, take pictures, or record the play. Use the pictures to make a class book, or watch the video together. Extensions: Actors can write the script themselves, or perform their play for an audience.

68.   **Scrambled Letters:** Put the letters of the animal's name on cards in the pocket of the animal's vest or gear bag. Have them draw out the letters and make as many words as they can out of those letters. See if they can put all of the cards together to make the animal's name.

69.   **Silly Sentences:** The client randomly selects two cards from a deck of animal-themed word cards and puts both in one sentence that makes sense. Students could write their sentences or share them verbally.

70.   **Story time:** The client snuggles with the animal partner while the professional reads an animal-themed book to them. The client could

also read the book to the animal. Provide a collection of animal-related books from which to choose. Extensions: Provide bookmarks with the animal's picture, or reading cards, where the readers get their card stamped each time they read to the animal, or are read to. When their card is filled, they get to take home a prize. See Appendix C for a list of animal-themed books.

71. **What's Next?** Have the client do an activity with the animal. Draw or take several pictures throughout the activity. Then have the client put the pictures in the order in which they happened. Extension: Have the students write a sentence for each picture, using sequence words such as first, next, then, etc.

72. **Word Book:** Depending on the part of speech being taught, the handler would position the animal partner in different places or doing different activities while the client or professional takes pictures of the animal. Make a book out of the pictures, writing the target words or sentences on the page. For example, if you're working on verbs, take a picture of the cat running, walking, sleeping, sitting, purring etc. If you're working on complete sentences, have them write a sentence with

a subject and predicate under the picture. This can be adapted for nouns, adjectives, adverbs, prepositions, subjects and predicates, second languages, etc.

73.   **Word Search:** Have the student put a treat in specific places using target vocabulary. Then the student uses the vocabulary to tell the animal partner where to find the treat. For example, if the goal is to use prepositions, the student hides the treat in, on, under, beside, or between props such as cups, bowls, or tables. Then the client uses those prepositions to tell the animal partner where to find the treat. This can be adapted to study other words such as nouns, speech sounds, adjectives or words in a second language.

Science

74.   **Adaptations:** Study the animal's physical and behavioral adaptations and explain how the adaptation helps the animal partner survive. Display them on a chart. Examples of adaptations are: the shape of their teeth, their sense of smell, their eyesight, their tendency to herd, fight, or cuddle, the shape of their head or body, their color, etc.

Adaptation	Physical or Behavioral	How does it help?
Bloodhound's long ears	Physical	When they sniff the ground, the ears fall down in front of its nose, holding in the scent
Birds lay eggs	Behavioral	They're able to fly easier without the weight of carrying their babies.

75. **Breeds:** Introduce the students to different breeds of animals. Have them research the purpose for which the animal partner's breed was bred, and what adaptations, both physical and behavioral they have to help them do what they were bred for. Extension: discuss the type of breed-related behaviors you might see from these breeds in present day society because of their history. For example, border collies were bred to herd sheep. They run low to the ground, they have a lot of energy, are very smart, and are self-driven. Border collies today often try to herd other dogs and their own family members. If not given a job, they use their energy to get into trouble!

76.   **Classification:** After learning about the characteristics of mammals, birds, reptiles, amphibians, and fish, have the students find those characteristics on the therapy animal. A mammal has hair, lungs, gives birth to live young, feeds them milk, has a backbone, and is warm-blooded. Birds have feathers, lungs, lay eggs, have hollow bones, a backbone, and are warm-blooded. Extensions: Students could also look for scales, gills, feathers, etc. to decide what type of animal the animal partner is. They could label these characteristics on a picture of the therapy animal.

77.   **Family Resemblance:** This works well if the handler has pictures of the therapy animal's mother and father. If not, look at pictures of other animal families. Discuss how traits are passed from generation to generation. You could also discuss how shelties have sheltie puppies, and Siamese cats will always have Siamese kittens. Show two animals and have the students predict what their babies might look like, or have them try to match pictures of the parents and babies. For advanced students, dominant and recessive genes, as well as the Punnett Square would be a great follow-up.

78.   **Germs:** Using Petri dishes, examine bacteria. Swab the animal's coat and rub it on a Petri dish. Do the same with the student's hair on a second Petri dish. Be sure to seal the Petri dishes at this point so clients aren't exposed to growing bacteria. Let the Petri dishes sit in a warm place for a few days and compare bacteria growth. Extensions: Test swabs of clients' feet and the animal partner's paws, human tongue and the animal partner's tongue, etc. Discuss the importance of hand washing and hygiene.

79.   **Head, Shoulders, Knees and Toes:** Work on naming the body parts. Have the child find them on herself, through her clothes, then point to the same part on the animal. Extensions: Have the child put a sticker on their own part. The client could also listen to the body parts with a stethoscope. Label the body parts on a picture of the animal.

80.   **Picky Eaters:** Define carnivores, herbivores, and omnivores. Offer the animal partner meats, fruits and vegetables. Label the animal partner and other animals as carnivores, herbivores, or omnivores.

81. **Research:** Have the client study the animal partner and think of a question that could be answered by research. Students can do research online, in books, or through personal observation and interviews. Examples of questions could be: how they care for their young; what type of food they eat; their roles in packs; how they communicate with each other; the history of the domestic animal; how their sense of smell works; when and why they shed; what sounds they make and what do they mean, etc. Then give a presentation, write a report, pamphlet, or PowerPoint slide show to teach others about what they've learned.

82. **Science Project:** Have the students think of a question they could answer by doing an experiment. Then have them follow the scientific method to prove their hypothesis. For example, if the student's question is, "Which toy do dogs prefer?" the student could offer the animal partner eight different toys in a box, 5 times throughout the visit. Collect data of which toy he chose each time. Use graphs, tables, a report, or PowerPoint to display the data. Some examples of questions are: Which collar works the best? Which kind of water bowl would he prefer? Do they see in color? How far away can a dog smell a treat? Which

type of treat would he prefer? Have them include other animals in their projects to add to their data pool and make their research more accurate.

83. **Touchy Feely:** Place a blindfold on the client and have him gently explore the animal partner by touch.

84. **Zoom In:** Have the students examine the animal partner with a magnifying glass or stethoscope.

Social Studies

85. **Careers:** After getting to know the therapy animal and handler, invite professionals from different animal-related careers, such as trainers, vets, groomers, dog sitters, vet techs, and animal-rescue workers to talk about their careers.

86. **Cultures:** Research the role that animals play in different cultures and compare them to the role that animals play in our own culture.

87. **Debate/Animal Issues:** Introduce controversial animal-related subjects and have the students practice respectful debate. Extension: Have them write letters to their local lawmakers. Ideas for topics could include: purebreeds vs. crossbreeds, domesticating wild animals as pets, spay and neutering, breeders and rescues, different training methods, docking ears and tails, puppy mills, animal rights, breed banning, current animal abuse laws, etc.

88. **Pack Dynamics:** Study pack dynamics: how groups of animals live together and cooperate. Define terms such as alpha, beta, dominant and submissive. Compare this to how the clients' own families cooperate.

Math

89. **Measure Me:** Measure different aspects of the animal. How much does he weigh? How tall/wide/long is he? What temperature is his armpit? What's the length of his tail? Ears? Hair? Paws? Toenails? How many times does he breathe in a minute?

90.   **Counting:** Have the child count the animal's spots, her whiskers, toenails, pads on her feet, eyes, or treats, etc.

91.   **Word Problems:** Have the students each write a mathematical story problem with the animal partner as the main character. On the back of the paper, write the answer. Then have the students trade papers and solve each others' problems. For example, "Fido has a box of twenty-four dog biscuits. He eats five of them. How many does he have left?"

Skill Practice

92.   **Step on It:** Spread flashcards out upside down on the floor. Have two or more students and the animal partner sit on the floor around the cards. The therapy animal's job is to select the card. Player 1 calls the animal partner who walks across the cards to get to him. Player 1 pets the animal partner and turns over the first card the animal stepped on. If he can answer the question on the card, he gets to keep it. Then player 2 calls the animal and the play continues. This can be used for any subject:

colors, phonics, math facts, shapes, science questions, speech sounds, sight words, vocabulary words, word families, etc.

93.   **Special Delivery:** Put prepared cards in the animal's vest or front pocket of the gear bag. Have the child randomly pull out a card and answer the question on the card. To make the activity more exciting, put a point value on each card. If the student gets the question right, they get the number of points on the card. This activity can be used for any subject: colors, phonics, math facts, shapes, science questions, speech sounds, sight words, vocabulary words, word families, etc.

94.   **Animal Genius:** This activity works well for children young enough not realize the dog has great scent skills. First have the handler turn the dog around, or leave the room. The professional puts a series of differently colored, upside-down cups on the floor. Have the child put a treat under the "red" cup. Then the handler brings the dog in. The child tells the dog that the treat's under the red cup. The dog goes straight to that cup. He's a genius! This can be adapted to practice colors, sizes, shapes, numbers, letters, speech sounds, math facts, etc. Just label identical cups with potential choices.

Add your own academic ideas here.

Service Projects

With so much need in our communities, it seems natural for able clients to participate in service projects. Some are coming to us with lifetimes of experience. Why not let them make a difference in the lives of others? Children too will gain a deep appreciation for the importance of service if they can have positive experiences serving others when they are young. Animals can inspire many creative ideas, including the few ideas mentioned here.

95. **Tug Toys:** Braid fleece strips together and knot them on the ends to make toys for the local animal shelter or rescue.

96. **Yarns:** Knit or crochet dog sweaters or cat toys. Patterns can be found at any fabric store. Donate them to the local animal shelter or rescue.

97. **Knots:** Provide a blanket-sized, animal-themed piece of fleece. Cut ½ -inch wide, 3-inch long fringes around the perimeter. Then tie a knot on each piece of fringe. Crate pads and beds can be made in a similar

way by putting two pieces of fleece on top of each other, with batting in the middle. Cut the fringes so the top and bottom pieces line up. Then tie the two layers together. Tie a few pieces of yarn in the middle, as if you were tying a quilt, to hold it together. Then donate them to a local animal shelter or rescue.

98. **Quilting:** Make quilts out of animal-themed fabric and donate or sell them to raise money for the local animal shelter or rescue.

99. **Grandparents:** Elderly adults can invite children to come to their facility for an hour of animal-related fun. Have the children read animal-themed books to the animal partners and Grandparent, do an art project, play a game, and eat a snack together. Children could also plan the activity and invite elderly adults.

100. **Fund Raiser:** Hold a donation drive for the local animal shelter or rescue. Advertise, collect supplies and money and donate everything to the good cause.

101. **Seeds:** Plant a garden with catnip and

wheatgrass. Cats enjoy rolling in, smelling, and eating the catnip, and many dogs and cats, as well as rabbits enjoy munching on wheatgrass. Dry the catnip and put it into homemade cat toys. Share them with the therapy team.

Add your own ideas for service projects here.

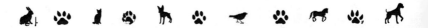

Goals

Goals are listed in the following categories:

- Physical

- Mental Health

- Social

- Cognitive/Academic

- Self Help/Occupational

- Speech

Sample goals within these categories are arranged in alphabetical order, followed by suggested interventions. Each intervention has a corresponding number to aid in quickly finding details and instructions in the first section of this book.

Physical Goals

Ambulation

Any activity that involves walking or running:

Dance Party (10)	Dog-Dog-Cat (11)
Fido Says (13)	Follow the Leader (15)
Going For a Walk (55)	Going Visiting (33)
Hide and Seek (16)	Lights Camera Action (67)
Musical Dots (19)	Obstacle Course (20)
Red Light Green Light (23)	Soccer (24)
Sportsmanship (36)	Word Search (73)

Balance

Any activity where the client is standing, sitting, or kneeling:

Animal Artists (48)	Animal Genius (94)
Beauty Parlor (31)	Blowing Bubbles (9)
Candid Camera (32)	Collage Art (49)

Dance Party (10)	Dog-Dog-Cat (11)
Fetch (12)	Fido Says (13)
Follow The Leader (15)	Gear Bag (40)
Going Visiting (33)	Grab Bag (14)
Grooming (2)	Hand Washing (62)
Hide and Seek (16)	Kitchen Time (61)
Lights, Camera, Action! (67)	Making Copies (50)
Measure Me (89)	Memory (17)
Movie and Popcorn (18)	Murals (51)
Musical Dots (19)	Nurturing (1)
Obstacle Course (20)	Off and Take It (21)
Offering Treats (5)	Paw Prints (52)
Peanut Butter (58)	Petting (6)
Preparing For a Walk (56)	Red Light Green Light (23)
Selecting Stuff (57)	Shape Up (53)
Sit and Share (35)	Sitting In A Garden (4)
Soccer (24)	Story Time (70)
Teaching Tricks (25)	The Cup Game (26)
Treasure Hunt (27)	Treat Hunt (28)
Tug Toys (95)	Yoga (60)
You Blew It! (30)	Zoom In (84)

Bilateral Coordination

Fine Motor:

Animal Artists (48)

Blowing Bubbles (9)

Collage Art (49)

Grab Bag (14)

Hand Washing (62)

Making Copies (50)

Murals (51)

Paw Prints (52)

Photo Album (41)

Shape Up (53)

Trendy T-shirts (54)

Up Close and Personal (3)

Beauty Parlor (31)

Candid Camera (32)

Gear Bag (40)

Grooming (2)

Kitchen Time (61)

Measure Me (89)

Nurturing (1)

Peanut Butter (58)

Preparing For a Walk (56)

Tiny Treats (63)

Tug Toys (95)

Gross Motor:

Yoga (60)

Going For A Walk (55)

Treasure Hunt (27)

Soccer (24)

Password (22)

Dog-Dog-Cat (11)

Follow The Leader (15)   Red Light Green Light (23)

Musical Dots (19)   Fido Says(13)

Going Visiting (33)

Body/Space Awareness

Any activity where the client moves in space or makes contact with
something or someone else:

Animal Artists (48)   Beauty Parlor (31)

Blowing Bubbles (9)   Candid Camera (32)

Dance Party (10)   Dog-Dog-Cat (11)

Eyes On Me (7)   Fetch (12)

Fido Says (13)   Follow The Leader (15)

Going For A Walk (55)   Grab Bag (14)

Grooming (2)   Hide and Seek (16)

Kitchen Time (61)   Lights, Camera, Action! (67)

Musical Dots (19)   Nurturing (1)

Obstacle Course (20)   Off and Take It (21)

Password (22)   Paw Prints (52)

Peanut Butter (58)   Petting (6)

Preparing For a Walk (56)   Red Light Green Light (23)

Crossing Midline

Position the animal partner and client in such a way that the client crosses midline:

Animal Artists (48)

Animal Genius (94)

Beauty Parlor (31)

Fetch (12)

Fido Says (13)

Follow The Leader (15)

Gear Bag (40)

Grab Bag (14)

Going Visiting *have the client reach across to knock on doors*

Grooming (2)

Kitchen Time (61)

Murals (51)

Nurturing (1)

Offering Treats (5)

Peanut Butter (58)

Petting (6)

Photo Album (41)

Preparing For a Walk (56)   Selecting Stuff (57)

Up Close and Personal (3)   What Now? (29)

Yoga (60)   Zoom In (84)

Endurance

Adjust the length of time and expenditure of energy to match the goal of the client:

Animal Artists (48)   Beauty Parlor (31)

Blowing Bubbles (9)   Dance Party (10)

Dog-Dog-Cat (11)   Fetch (12)

Fido Says (13)   Follow The Leader (15)

Going For A Walk (55)   Going Visiting (33)

Grooming (2)   Hide and Seek (16)

Kitchen Time (61)   Murals (51)

Musical Dots (19)   Obstacle Course (20)

Off and Take It (21)   Petting (6)

Red Light Green Light (23)   Service Projects (95-101)

Sit and Share (35)   Sitting In A Garden (4)

Soccer (24)   The Cup Game (26)

Treasure Hunt (27)   Trendy T-shirts (54)

Up Close and Personal (3)   Yoga (60)

You Blew It! (30)

Eye/Hand Coordination

Animal Artists (48)   Animal Bingo (8)

Animal Genius (94)   Authors (64)

Beauty Parlor (31)   Blowing Bubbles (9)

Candid Camera (32)   Chores (38)

Collage Art (49)   Dog-Dog-Cat (11)

Eyes On Me (7)   Fetch (12)

Gear Bag (40)   Grooming (2)

Hide and Seek (16)   Kitchen Time (61)

Knots (97)   Making Copies (50)

Measure Me (89)   Murals (51)

Nurturing (1)   Off and Take It (21)

Offering Treats (5)   Password (22)

Paw Prints (52)   Peanut Butter (58)

Petting (6)   Photo Album (41)

Preparing For a Walk(56)   Selecting Stuff (57)

Service Projects (95-101)   Shape Up (53)

Silly Sentences (69)   Special Delivery (93)

Fine Motor Skills

Grasping Skills

Tug Toys (95)   What Now? (29)

Zoom In (84)

Inattention to Weak Side of Body

Tweak the intervention so the client must use the weak side of the body to complete the activity:

Animal Bingo (8)   Beauty Parlor (31)

Blowing Bubbles (9)   Chores (38)

Eyes On Me (7)   Fetch (12)

Fido Says (13)   Follow The Leader (15)

Gear Bag (40)   Going For A Walk (55)

Grooming (2)   Hand Washing (62)

Nurturing (1)   Offering Treats (5)

Paw Prints (52)   Petting (6)

Preparing For a Walk (56)   Selecting Stuff (57)

Soccer (24)   Teaching Tricks (25)

The Cup Game (26)   Treasure Hunt (27)

Treat Hunt (28)   Up Close and Personal (3)

What Now? (29)   Yoga (60)

Posture

Posture can be addressed while doing any sitting or standing activity:

Animal Artists (48)	Animal Bingo (8)
Animal Genius (94)	Beauty Parlor (31)
Blowing Bubbles (9)	Candid Camera (32)
Collage Art (49)	Dance Party (10)
Dog-Dog-Cat (11)	Eyes On Me (7)
Fetch (12)	Fido Says (13)
Follow The Leader (15)	Gear Bag (40)
Going Visiting (33)	Grooming (2)
Hide and Seek (16)	Kitchen Time (61)
Making Copies (50)	Memory (17)
Movie and Popcorn (18)	Murals (51)
Musical Dots (19)	Nurturing (1)
Obstacle Course (20)	Off and Take It (21)
Offering Treats (5)	Paw Prints (52)
Peanut Butter (58)	Petting (6)
Photo Album (41)	Preparing For a Walk (56)
Red Light Green Light (23)	Reminiscing (42)
Selecting Stuff (57)	Shape Up (53)
Sit and Share (35)	Sitting In A Garden (4)

Soccer (24)

Teaching Tricks (25)

Tiny Treats (63)

Treat Hunt (28)

Tug Toys (95)

Yoga (60)

Story Time (70)

The Cup Game (26)

Treasure Hunt (27)

Trendy T-shirts (54)

Up Close and Personal (3)

You Blew It! (30)

Range of Motion

Animal Genius (94)

Blowing Bubbles (9)

Dog-Dog-Cat (11)

Fido Says (13)

Gear Bag (40)

Measure Me (89)

Nurturing (1)

Offering Treats (5)

Preparing For a Walk (56)

Soccer (24)

Treat Hunt (28)

What Now? (29)

Beauty Parlor (31)

Chores (38)

Fetch (12)

Follow The Leader (15)

Grooming (2)

Murals (51)

Off and Take It (21)

Petting (6)

Selecting Stuff (57)

Treasure Hunt (27)

Up Close and Personal (3)

Yoga (60)

Releasing Objects

Animal Artists (48)

Beauty Parlor (31)

Candid Camera (32)

Eyes On Me (7)

Gear Bag (40)

Grooming (2)

Kitchen Time (61)

Nurturing (1)

Offering Treats (5)

Preparing For a Walk (56)

Service Projects (95-101)

Tiny Treats (63)

Treat Hunt (28)

What Now? (29)

Animal Genius (94)

Blowing Bubbles (9)

Chores (38)

Fetch (12)

Grab Bag (14)

Hide and Seek (16)

Measure Me (89)

Off and Take It (21)

Picky Eaters (80)

Selecting Stuff (57)

The Cup Game (26)

Treasure Hunt (27)

Teaching Tricks (25)

Word Search (73)

Strength

An option is to add arm or leg weights while doing these activities, with particular care given to safety:

Animal Artists (48)

Blowing Bubbles (9)

Dance Party (10)

Fetch (12)

Fido Says (13)

Follow The Leader (15)

Gear Bag (40)

Grooming (2)

Kitchen Time (61)

Murals (51)

Off and Take It (21)

Offering Treats (5)

Peanut Butter (58)

Petting (6)

Soccer (24)

The Cup Game (26)

Treasure Hunt (27)

Treat Hunt (28)

Yoga (60)

Tactile Stimulation

Animal Artists (48)

Dog-Dog-Cat (11)

Fetch (12)

Gear Bag (40)

Grooming (2)

Hand Washing (62)

Kitchen Time (61)

Nurturing(1)

Off and Take It (21)

Paw Prints (52)

Petting (6)

Touchy Feely (83)

Up Close and Personal (3)

Sit and Share (35)

Treasure Hunt (27)

Transferring From Bed/Chair/Couch, Etc

Stage any activity in a place different from where the client is. This alone will give the client motivation to transfer positions.

Visual Tracking

Animal Genius (94)

Candid Camera (32)

Eyes On Me (7)

Blowing Bubbles (9)

Dog-Dog-Cat (11)

Fetch (12)

Head, Shoulders, Knees and Toes (79)

Hide and Seek (16)

Offering Treats (5)

Sit and Share (35)

Teaching Tricks (25)

Treat Hunt (28)

Word Search (73)

Off and Take It (21)

Photo Album (41)

Soccer (24)

The Cup Game (26)

Word Book (72)

You Blew It! (30)

Use this space to add physical goals of your own.

Mental Health Goals

Anxiety

Some of these interventions can directly address anxiety, others provide quality time with an animal partner, creative expression, and service, all of which can help to relieve anxiety.

Animal Artists (48)

Authors (64)

Blowing Bubbles (9)

Commonalities (39)

Going For a Walk (55)

Going Visiting (33)

Grooming (2)

Nurturing (1)

Offering Treats (5)

Petting (6)

Reminiscing (42)

Service Projects (95-101)

Sit and Share (35)

Sitting In a Garden (4)

Staying Safe (43)

Story Time (70)

Treat Hunt (28)

Teaching Tricks (25)

Up Close and Personal (3)

Yoga (60)

Attention Span

Any activity that takes a certain amount of time can address attention span. Adjust the length of the activity to match the client's goal.

20 Questions (47)

Animal Artists (48)

Authors (64)

Blowing Bubbles (9)

Counting (90)

Eyes On Me (7)

Fido Says (13)

Gear Bag (40)

Going Visiting (33)

Grooming (2)

Kitchen Time (61)

Making Copies (50)

Memory (17)

Murals (51)

Nurturing (1)

Off and Take It (21)

Password (22)

Petting (6)

Adaptations (74)

Animal Bingo (8)

Beauty Parlor (31)

Collage Art (49)

Dog-Dog-Cat (11)

Fetch (12)

Follow The Leader (15)

Going For A Walk (55)

Grab Bag (14)

Hide and Seek (16)

Lights, Camera, Action! (67)

Measure Me (89)

Movie and Popcorn (18)

Musical Dots (19)

Obstacle Course (20)

Offering Treats (5)

Peanut Butter (58)

Photo Album (41)

Preparing For a Walk (56)

Selecting Stuff (57)

Sit and Share (35)

Story Time (70)

The Cup Game (26)

Treasure Hunt (27)

Trivia (46)

Yoga (60)

Zoom In (84)

Reminiscing (42)

Service Projects (95-101)

Soccer (24)

Teaching Tricks (25)

Translations (45)

Treat Hunt (28)

Up Close and Personal (3)

You Blew It! (30)

Depression

Some of these interventions can directly address depression and the issues associated with it. Others activities give the client opportunities for positive experiences.

Beauty Parlor (31)

Candid Camera (32)

Dance Party (10)

Going For A Walk (55)

Good Friends (34)

Hide and Seek (16)

Peanut Butter (58)

Blowing Bubbles (9)

Commonalities (39)

Fetch (12)

Going Visiting (33)

Grooming (2)

Nurturing (1)

Petting (6)

Reminiscing (42)

Sit and Share (35)

Stressin' (44)

The Cup Game (26)

Treat Hunt (28)

Yoga (60)

Service Projects (95-101)

Sitting In A Garden (4)

Teaching Tricks (25)

Translations (45)

Up Close and Personal (3)

Emotional Regulation

Some of these interventions can address emotional regulation directly, others give the client an opportunity to practice regulating emotion.

Animal Bingo (8)

Debate/Animal Issues (87)

Fetch (12)

Going Visiting (33)

Hide and Seek (16)

Musical Dots (19)

Password (22)

Sit and Share (35)

Stressin' (44)

The Cup Game (26)

Treasure Hunt (27)

Commonalities (39)

Dog-Dog-Cat (11)

Fido Says (13)

Good Friends (34)

Memory (17)

Pack Dynamics (88)

Red Light Green Light (23)

Sportsmanship (36)

Teaching Tricks (25)

Translations (45)

Expressing Emotion

Some of these interventions can address expressing emotion directly, others are meant to give the client an opportunity to practice expressing emotion.

Animal Bingo (8)	Authors (64)
Candid Camera (32)	Commonalities (39)
Debate/Animal Issues (87)	Dog-Dog-Cat (11)
Fido Says (13)	Good Friends (34)
Lights, Camera, Action! (67)	Memory (17)
Musical Dots (19)	Nurturing (1)
Obstacle Course (20)	Off and Take It (21)
Password (22)	Petting (6)
Photo Album (41)	Reminiscing (42)
Sit and Share (35)	Soccer (24)
Sportsmanship (36)	Stressin' (44)
Teaching Tricks (25)	Thanks (37)
The Cup Game (26)	Translations (45)
Treasure Hunt (27)	Treat Hunt (28)
Up Close and Personal (3)	

Grieving Process

Animals are very good at just being there with someone who is grieving. Many of these interventions allow for that. Others can directly address grief.

Commonalities (39)

Grooming (2)

Petting (6)

Service Projects (95-101)

Stressin' (44)

Up Close and Personal (3)

Going For a Walk (55)

Nurturing (1)

Reminiscing (42)

Sitting In A Garden (4)

Translations (45)

Loneliness

Most of these interventions allow the animal partner to instigate social interaction. Others provide quality time with the animal, and some can directly address loneliness.

Animal Bingo (8)

Blowing Bubbles (9)

Commonalities (39)

Dog-Dog-Cat (11)

Going For A Walk (55)

Good Friends (34)

Beauty Parlor (31)

Candid Camera (32)

Dance Party (10)

Fetch (12)

Going Visiting (33)

Grooming (2)

Hide and Seek (16)

Off and Take It (21)

Petting (6)

Red Light Green Light (23)

Service Projects (95-101)

Soccer (24)

The Cup Game (26)

Treat Hunt (28)

You Blew It! (30)

Nurturing (1)

Offering Treats (5)

Photo Album (41)

Reminiscing (42)

Sit and Share (35)

Teaching Tricks (25)

Translations (45)

Up Close and Personal (3)

Memory/Recall

20 Questions (47)

Animal Genius (94)

Compare and Contrast (65)

Gear Bag (40)

Going Visiting *(client remembers which rooms to visit)* (33)

Hide and Seek (16)

Password (22)

Selecting Stuff (57)

Special Delivery (93)

Word Search (73)

Adaptations (74)

Candid Camera (32)

Counting (90)

Grab Bag (14)

Memory (17)

Reminiscing (42)

Service Projects (95-101)

Trivia (46)

Reality Orientation

Beauty Parlor (31)

Blowing Bubbles (9)

Candid Camera (32)

Dog-Dog-Cat (11)

Eyes On Me (7)

Fetch (12)

Fido Says (13)

Gear Bag (40)

Going For A Walk (55)

Going Visiting (33)

Grooming (2)

Hand Washing (62)

Hide and Seek (16)

Kitchen Time (61)

Nurturing (1)

Obstacle Course (20)

Off and Take It (21)

Offering Treats (5)

Peanut Butter (58)

Petting (6)

Photo Album (41)

Preparing For a Walk (56)

Red Light Green Light (23)

Selecting Stuff (57)

Service Projects (95-101)

Sit and Share (35)

Sitting In A Garden (4)

Soccer (24)

Teaching Tricks (25)

The Cup Game (26)

Tiny Treats (63)

Tongue-ersize (59)

Translations (45)

Treasure Hunt (27)

Treat Hunt (28)

Up Close and Personal (3)

What Now? (29)

Word Book (72)

Word Search (73)

You Blew It! (30)

Zoom In (84)

Restlessness

Some of these interventions can address restlessness directly. Others provide physical activity or artistic expression.

Animal Artists (48)

Authors (64)

Beauty Parlor (31)

Blowing Bubbles (9)

Commonalities (39)

Fetch (12)

Fido Says (13)

Follow The Leader (15)

Going For A Walk (55)

Going Visiting (33)

Grooming (2)

Kitchen Time (61)

Murals (51)

Musical Dots (19)

Nurturing (1)

Petting (6)

Photo Album (41)

Reminiscing (42)

Service Projects (95-101)

Sit and Share (35)

Sitting In A Garden (4)

Stressin' (44)

Up Close and Personal (3)

Yoga (60)

Self Esteem

Many of these activities allow for a client to practice and master a skill.
Others allow the animal partner to spend quality time with the client.

Animal Artists (48)

Authors (64)

Beauty Parlor (31)

Candid Camera (32)

Commonalities (39)

Fetch (12)

Follow The Leader (15)

Going Visiting (33)

Good Friends (34)

Grab Bag (14)

Grooming (2)

Hide and Seek (16)

Kitchen Time (61)

Lights, Camera, Action! (67)

Murals (51)

Nurturing (1)

Obstacle Course (20)

Off and Take It (21)

Offering Treats (5)

Password (22)

Petting (6)

Preparing For a Walk (56)

Reminiscing (42)

Service Projects (95-101)

Shape Up (53)

Sit and Share (35)

Soccer (24)

Stressin' (44)

Teaching Tricks (25)

Thanks (37)

Translations (45)

Trendy T-shirts (54)

Up Close and Personal (3)

What Now? (29)

Trust

These activities allow the animal partner to earn the client's trust, and the client to earn the animal's trust. A few also directly address trust issues.

Chores (38)

Commonalities (39)

Eyes On Me (7)

Fetch (12)

Going For A Walk (55)

Going Visiting (33)

Good Friends (34)

Grooming (2)

Hide and Seek (16)

Nurturing (1)

Obstacle Course (20)

Off and Take It (21)

Offering Treats (5)

Petting (6)

Photo Album (41)

Reminiscing (42)

Soccer (24)

Staying Safe (43)

Story Time (70)

Teaching Tricks (25)

Thanks (37)

Translations (45)

Up Close and Personal (3)

Use this space to add mental health goals of your own!

Social Goals

Appropriate Touch (receiving and giving)

Beauty Parlor (31)

Commonalities (39)

Dance Party (10)

Dog-Dog-Cat (11)

Grooming (2)

Measure Me (89)

Head, Shoulders, Knees and Toes (79)

Nurturing (1)

Petting (6)

Preparing For a Walk (56)

Sit and Share (35)

Touchy Feely (83)

Translations (45)

Up Close and Personal (3)

Yoga (60)

Zoom In (84)

Constructive Criticism (receiving and offering)

These activities offer opportunities for the professional and client to offer and accept constructive criticism:

Adaptations (74)

Animal Genius (94)

Authors (64)

Beauty Parlor (31)

Blowing Bubbles (9)

Debate/Animal Issues (87)

Fido Says (13)

Grooming (2)

Kitchen Time (61)

Making Copies (50)

Obstacle Course (20)

Password (22)

Peanut Butter (58)

Red Light Green Light (23)

Silly Sentences (69)

Story Time (70)

Teaching Tricks (25)

Translations (45)

Trendy T-shirts (54)

Commonalities (39)

Eyes On Me (7)

Good Friends (34)

Hide and Seek (16)

Lights, Camera, Action! (67)

Murals (51)

Off and Take It (21)

Paw Prints (52)

Preparing For a Walk (56)

Service Projects (95-101)

Soccer (24)

Stressin' (44)

Tongue-ersize (59)

Treasure Hunt (27)

You Blew It! (30)

Cooperation

These activities require cooperation between the client and the animal partner in order to succeed.

Beauty Parlor (31)

Candid Camera (32)

Blowing Bubbles (9)

Chores (38)

Commonalities (39)

Follow The Leader (15)

Going Visiting (33)

Hide and Seek (16)

Lights, Camera, Action! (67)

Murals (51)

Off and Take It (21)

Pack Dynamics (88)

Peanut Butter (58)

Service Projects (95-101)

Teaching Tricks (25)

The Cup Game (26)

Trendy T-shirts (54)

Fetch (12)

Going For A Walk (55)

Good Friends (34)

Kitchen Time (61)

Measure Me (89)

Obstacle Course (20)

Offering Treats (5)

Password (22)

Preparing For a Walk (56)

Soccer (24)

Thanks (37)

Translations (45)

What Now? (29)

Eye Contact

These activities incorporate eye contact between the client and other people as well as between the client and the animal partner.

20 Questions (47)

Commonalities (39)

Eyes On Me (7)

Grooming (2)

Candid Camera (32)

Debate/Animal Issues (87)

Going Visiting (33)

Nurturing (1)

Offering Treats (5)   Petting (6)

Reminiscing (42)   Selecting Stuff (57)

Service Projects (95-101)   Sit and Share (35)

Stressin' (44)   Teaching Tricks (25)

Thanks (37)   Translations (45)

Trivia (46)   Up Close and Personal (3)

Help - Offering and Accepting

These interventions provide opportunities to help others, help the animal partner, and receive help from others.

Animal Genius (94)   Beauty Parlor (31)

Candid Camera (32)   Chores (38)

Collage Art (49)   Commonalities (39)

Counting (90)   Eyes On Me (7)

Going For A Walk (55)   Grooming (2)

Hand Washing (62)   Hide and Seek (16)

Kitchen Time (61)   Lights, Camera, Action! (67)

Making Copies (50)   Measure Me (89)

Memory (17)   Murals (51)

Nurturing (1)   Obstacle Course (20)

Offering Treats (5)   Pack Dynamics (88)

Password (22)

Preparing For a Walk (56)

Shape Up (53)

Staying Safe (43)

Teaching Tricks (25)

Treasure Hunt (27)

Trendy T-shirts (54)

Yoga (60)

Paw Prints (52)

Service Projects (95-101)

Soccer (24)

Story Time (70)

Touchy Feely (83)

Treat Hunt (28)

What Now? (29)

You Blew It! (30)

Making Choices

Have the client choose which activity to do, as well as the details of the following activities.

20 Questions (47)

Authors (64)

Candid Camera (32)

Collage Art (49)

Dog-Dog-Cat (11)

Going For A Walk (55)

Grab Bag (14)

Hide and Seek (16)

Nurturing (1)

Animal Artists (48)

Beauty Parlor (31)

Careers (85)

Debate/Animal Issues (87)

Follow The Leader (15)

Going Visiting (33)

Grooming (2)

Musical Dots (19)

Obstacle Course (20)

Off and Take It (21)

Paw Prints (52)

Selecting Stuff (57)

Shape Up (53)

Story Time (70)

Trendy T-shirts (54)

What Now? (29)

Offering Treats (5)

Picky Eaters (80)

Service Projects (95-101)

Silly Sentences (69)

Teaching Tricks (25)

Trivia (46)

Word Search (73)

Manipulative Behaviors

Any of these activities offer practice in not being manipulative. When manipulative behaviors present themselves, the professional should be ready to help the client recognize and change the behavior.

20 Questions (47)

Blowing Bubbles (9)

Commonalities (39)

Fetch (12)

Going Visiting (33)

Grab Bag (14)

Hide and Seek (16)

Offering Treats (5)

Password (22)

Animal Bingo (8)

Candid Camera (32)

Dog-Dog-Cat (11)

Fido Says (13)

Good Friends (34)

Grooming (2)

Musical Dots (19)

Pack Dynamics (88)

Red Light Green Light (23)

Service Projects (95-101)

Sit and Share (35)

Sportsmanship (36)

Stressin' (44)

The Cup Game (26)

Translations (45)

Treasure Hunt (27)

Treat Hunt (28)

Teaching Tricks (25)

Trivia (46)

Up Close and Personal (3)

What Now? (29)

Praise - Receiving and Offering

In these activities, praise can be given to the client, or the client can give praise to the animal. The handler can also "interpret" the animal's praise for the client.

20 Questions (47)

Animal Artists (48)

Animal Genius (94)

Authors (64)

Beauty Parlor (31)

Blowing Bubbles (9)

Candid Camera (32)

Chores (38)

Collage Art (49)

Commonalities (39)

Compare and Contrast (65)

Dance Party (10)

Debate/Animal Issues (87)

Eyes On Me (7)

Fetch (12)

Fido Says (13)

Follow The Leader (15)

Gear Bag (40)

Going Visiting (33)

Grab Bag (14)

Sharing/Turn Taking

Animal Genius(94)

Blowing Bubbles (9)

Commonalities (39)

Dog-Dog-Cat (11)

Follow The Leader (15)

Grab Bag (14)

Hide and Seek (16)

Obstacle Course (20)

Pack Dynamics (88)

Paw Prints (52)

Reminiscing (42)

Sit and Share (35)

Special Delivery (93)

The Cup Game (26)

Treasure Hunt (27)

You Blew It! (30)

Beauty Parlor (31)

Candid Camera (32)

Dance Party (10)

Fetch (12)

Going Visiting (33)

Hand Washing (62)

Nurturing (1)

Off and Take It (21)

Password (22)

Photo Album (41)

Selecting Stuff (57)

Soccer (24)

Step on It (92)

Tongue-ersize (59)

What Now? (29)

Zoom In (84)

Showing Appreciation

Clients can show appreciation to the animal, professional and handler, and the professional and animal partner (translated through the handler) can show appreciation to the client.

Animal Artists (48)

Beauty Parlor (31)

Candid Camera (32)

Chores (38)

Dance Party (10)

Going Visiting (33)

Grooming (2)

Kitchen Time (61)

Making Copies (50)

Obstacle Course (20)

Password (22)

Petting (6)

Reminiscing (42)

Service Projects (95-101)

Soccer (24)

Story Time (70)

Animal Bingo (8)

Blowing Bubbles (9)

Careers (85)

Commonalities (39)

Going For A Walk (55)

Good Friends (34)

Hide and Seek (16)

Lights, Camera, Action! (67)

Nurturing (1)

Off and Take It (21)

Peanut Butter (58)

Preparing For a Walk (56)

Selecting Stuff (57)

Sit and Share (35)

Special Delivery (93)

Thanks (37)

Tiny Treats (63) Trendy T-shirts (54)

Up Close and Personal (3) You Blew It! (30)

Social Interaction/Building Relationships

Many of these activities are great to do in groups, others can directly address social skills.

Animal Bingo (8) Beauty Parlor (31)

Blowing Bubbles (9) Candid Camera (32)

Commonalities (39) Dance Party (10)

Debate/Animal Issues (87) Dog-Dog-Cat (11)

Eyes On Me (7) Fetch (12)

Fido Says (13) Follow The Leader (15)

Going For A Walk (55) Going Visiting (33)

Good Friends (34) Grooming (2)

Hide and Seek (16) Kitchen Time (61)

Lights, Camera, Action! (67) Movie and Popcorn (18)

Musical Dots (19) Nurturing (1)

Obstacle Course (20) Off and Take It (21)

Offering Treats (5) Pack Dynamics (88)

Password (22) Peanut Butter (58)

Petting (6) Photo Album (41)

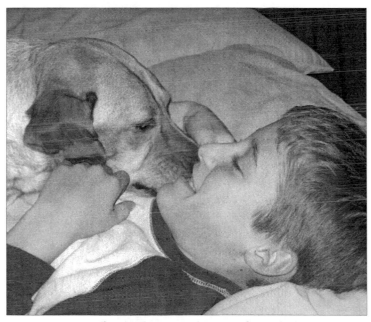

#21 Off and Take It ... A client giggles as Gracie takes a treat from above his shoulder.

Use this space to add social goals of your own.

Cognitive/Academic Goals

Concentration/Attention Span

Adjust the length and energy of the activities to match the clients' goals.

20 Questions (47)

Animal Artists (48)

Animal Genius (94)

Beauty Parlor (31)

Breeds (75)

Careers (85)

Collage Art (49)

Debate/Animal Issues (87)

Eyes On Me (7)

Fetch (12)

Follow The Leader (15)

Going For A Walk (55)

Adaptations (74)

Animal Bingo (8)

Authors (64)

Blowing Bubbles (9)

Candid Camera (32)

Classification (76)

Compare and Contrast (65)

Dog-Dog-Cat (11)

Fact and Opinion (66)

Fido Says (13)

Gear Bag (40)

Going Visiting (33)

Career Education

Cause and Effect

Adaptations (74)	Animal Bingo (8)
Authors (64)	Beauty Parlor (31)
Blowing Bubbles (9)	Breeds (75)
Chores (38)	Commonalities (39)
Debate/Animal Issues (87)	Dog-Dog-Cat (11)
Eyes On Me (7)	Fetch (12)
Fido Says (13)	Follow The Leader (15)
Gear Bag (40)	Germs (78)
Going Visiting (33)	Good Friends (34)
Grooming (2)	Hand Washing (62)
Hide and Seek (16)	Lights, Camera, Action! (67)
Musical Dots (19)	Nurturing (1)
Off and Take It (21)	Offering Treats (5)
Pack Dynamics (88)	Petting (6)
Red Light Green Light (23)	Reminiscing (42)
Science Project (82)	Service Projects (95-101)
Sit and Share (35)	Soccer (24)
Sportsmanship (36)	Staying Safe (43)
Story Time (70)	Teaching Tricks (25)

Directions - Following and Giving

Memory/Recall

Language Arts – Alphabet, Spelling and Phonics Skills

Animal Genius (94)	Musical Dots (19)
Password (22)	Scrambled Letters (68)
Selecting Stuff (57)	Special Delivery (93)
Step on It (92)	Story Time (70)
What Now? (29)	Word Book (72)
Word Problems (91)	Word Search (73)

Language Arts - Reading Comprehension Skills

Write the instructions for any activity and have the students read them before doing the activity. Some of these interventions practice reading comprehension strategies. Others require the client to read and comprehend.

Breeds (75)	Classification (76)
Commonalities (39)	Compare and Contrast (65)
Cultures (86)	Fact and Opinion (66)
Kitchen Time (61)	Lights, Camera, Action! (67)
Pack Dynamics (88)	Photo Album (41)
Reminiscing (42)	Research (81)

Language Arts – Reading Fluency

Language Arts - Grammar/Parts of Speech

Language Arts – Writing

Have the client write about doing any chosen activity. The following activities directly address writing.

Animal Bingo(8)

Compare and Contrast (65)

Fact and Opinion (66)

Lights, Camera, Action! (67)

Research (81)

Silly Sentences (69)

What's Next? (71)

Word Problems (91)

Authors (64)

Cultures (86)

Good Friends (34)

Pack Dynamics (88)

Science Project (82)

Thanks (37)

Word Book (72)

Math – Counting

The client can count the strokes, throws, seconds, steps, items, or points.

20 Questions (47)

Counting (90)

Grooming (2)

Hide and Seek (16)

Measure Me (89)

Off and Take It (21)

Animal Genius (94)

Fetch (12)

Hand Washing (62)

Kitchen Time (61)

Musical Dots (19)

Password (22)

Math – Geometry

Animal Genius (94)

Going For a Walk (55) *walk the perimeter of different shapes or find in the environment while walking*

Kitchen Time (61) *use cookie cutters to cut into different shapes*

Murals (51)

Musical Dots (19)

Password (22)

Peanut Butter (58) *use multi-shaped crackers or cut bread into different shapes before spreading*

Photo Album (41) *find different shapes in the pictures*

Shape Up (53)

Step on It (92)

Word Search (73)

Special Delivery (93)

Word Book (72)

Math – Graphing Data

Clients can collect data such as the seconds needed to complete an activity, measurements, or results of experiments, and graph the data.

Classification (76)   Compare and Contrast (65)

Family Resemblance (77)   Fetch (12)

Hide and Seek (16)   Measure Me (89)

Memory (17)   Murals (51)

Obstacle Course (20)   Off and Take It (21)

Picky Eaters (80)   Research (81)

Science Project (82)   Treasure Hunt (27)

Treat Hunt (28)

Math – Measurement

Fetch (12)   Kitchen Time (61)

Measure Me (89)   Murals (51)

Peanut Butter *measure before spreading* (58)

Special Delivery (93)   Word Problems (91)

Math - Memorizing Math Facts

Animal Genius (94)

Musical Dots (19)

Special Delivery (93)

Step on It (92)

Tiny Treats (63)

Math – Probability

Animal Bingo (8)

Animal Genius (94)

Dog-Dog-Cat (11)

Grab Bag (14)

Memory (17)

Musical Dots (19)

Special Delivery (93)

Step on It (92)

Math - Word Problems

Kitchen Time (61)

Special Delivery (93)

Step on It (92)

Tiny Treats (63)

Word Book (72)

Word Problems (91)

Physical Education

Dance Party (10)

Dog-Dog-Cat (11)

Fetch (12)

Fido Says (13)

Follow The Leader (15)

Going For A Walk (55)

Hide and Seek (16)

Musical Dots (19)

Obstacle Course (20)

Red Light Green Light (23)

Soccer (24)

Sportsmanship (36)

Yoga (60)

Second Language Learning

Preteach the vocabulary, then do any of the activities in the target language.

20 Questions (47)

Adaptations (74)

Animal Bingo (8)

Animal Genius (94)

Authors (64)

Beauty Parlor (31)

Candid Camera (32)

Careers (85)

Chores (38)

Classification (76)

Commonalities (39)

Compare and Contrast (65)

Cultures (86)

Dog-Dog-Cat (11)

Eyes On Me (7)

Fact and Opinion (66)

Fetch (12)

Fido Says (13)

Gear Bag (40)

Going Visiting (33)

Grab Bag (14)

Grooming (2)

Head, Shoulders, Knees and Toes (79)

Hide and Seek (16)

Lights, Camera, Action! (67)

Memory (17)

Musical Dots (19)

Obstacle Course (20)

Offering Treats (5)

Peanut Butter (58)

Picky Eaters (80)

Reminiscing (42)

Service Projects (95-101)

Soccer (24)

Staying Safe (43)

Story Time (70)

The Cup Game (26)

Treat Hunt (28)

Trivia (46)

What's Next? (71)

Word Search (73)

Kitchen Time (61)

Measure Me (89)

Movie and Popcorn (18)

Nurturing (1)

Off and Take It (21)

Password (22)

Photo Album (41)

Preparing For a Walk (56)

Scrambled Letters (68)

Silly Sentences (69)

Special Delivery (93)

Step on It (92)

Thanks (37)

Treasure Hunt (27)

Trendy T-shirts (54)

What Now? (29)

Word Book (72)

You Blew It! (30)

Science - 5 Senses

Some of these activities offer the opportunity for the clients to use their senses, others offer the opportunity for the client to observe the animal partner using her senses.

Adaptations (74)

Animal Genius (94)

Blowing Bubbles (9)

Dance Party (10)

Fetch (12)

Germs (78)

Grab Bag (14)

Hand Washing (62)

Kitchen Time (61)

Movie and Popcorn (18)

Obstacle Course (20)

Password (22)

Peanut Butter (58)

Red Light Green Light (23)

Science Project (82)

The Cup Game (26)

Touchy Feely (83)

Animal Artists (48)

Beauty Parlor (31)

Collage Art (49)

Eyes On Me (7)

Follow The Leader (15)

Going For A Walk (55)

Grooming (2)

Hide and Seek (16)

Measure Me (89)

Musical Dots (19)

Offering Treats (5)

Paw Prints (52)

Petting (6)

Research (81)

Sitting In A Garden (4)

Tongue-ersize (59)

Treasure Hunt (27)

Treat Hunt (28)   Up Close and Personal (3)

Zoom In (84)

Science - Animal Adaptations

Many of these activities require the animal partner to use its adaptations. Others allow students to study them.

Adaptations (74)   Animal Genius(94)

Breeds (75)   Classification (76)

Collage Art (49)   Compare and Contrast (65)

Cultures (86)   Fact and Opinion (66)

Family Resemblance (77)   Hide and Seek (16)

Head, Shoulders, Knees and Toes (79)

Measure Me (89)   Password (22)

Paw Prints (52)   Picky Eaters (80)

Research (81)   Science Project (82)

Story Time (70)   Stressin' (44)

The Cup Game (26)   Translations (45)

Treasure Hunt (27)   Treat Hunt (28)

Word Book (72)   Zoom In (84)

Science - Animal Behavior

Adaptations (74)	Breeds (75)
Classification (76)	Collage Art (49)
Fact and Opinion (66)	Family Resemblance (77)
Fetch (12)	Hide and Seek (16)
Pack Dynamics (88)	Research (81)
Science Project (82)	Sportsmanship (36)
Story Time (70)	Stressin' (44)
Translations (45)	Treasure Hunt (27)

Science - Body Parts

Adaptations (74)	Breeds (75)
Classification (76)	Collage Art (49)
Counting (90)	Family Resemblance (77)
Fido Says (13)	Germs (78)
Grooming (2)	Measure Me (89)

Head, Shoulders, Knees and Toes (79)

Off and Take It (21)	Password (22)
Paw Prints (52)	Preparing For a Walk (56)
Teaching Tricks (25)	Touchy Feely (83)
Word Book (72)	Zoom In (84)

Science – Colors

Animal Artists (48)	Animal Genius (94)
Blowing Bubbles (9)	Collage Art (49)
Knots (97)	Making Copies (50)
Murals (51)	Musical Dots (19)
Paw Prints (52)	Red Light Green Light (23)
Selecting Stuff (57)	Shape Up (53)
Sitting In A Garden (4)	Special Delivery (93)
Step on It (92)	Treasure Hunt (27)
Trendy T-shirts (54)	Tug Toys (95)
Word Book (72)	Word Search (73)
Zoom In (84)	

Science - Heredity/Genetics

Adaptations (74)	Breeds (75)
Classification(76)	Collage Art (49)
Family Resemblance (77)	Measure Me (89)
Head Shoulders Knees and Toes (79)	
Pack Dynamics (88)	Paw Prints (52)
Photo Album (41)	Research (81)
Science Project (82)	Stressin' (44)
Translations (45)	

Science - Animal Classification

Animal Bingo (8)

Breeds (75)

Collage Art (49)

Fact and Opinion (66)

Musical Dots (19)

Photo Album (41)

Research (81)

Special Delivery (93)

Treasure Hunt (27)

Zoom In (84)

Animal Genius (94)

Classification (76)

Compare and Contrast (65)

Family Resemblance (77)

Password (22)

Picky Eaters (80)

Science Project (82)

Step on It (92)

Word Book (72)

Science - Scientific Process

These activities provide opportunities for students to use the scientific process.

Breeds (75)

Germs (78)

Pack Dynamics (88)

Picky Eaters (80)

Teaching Tricks (25)

Family Resemblance (77)

Measure Me (89)

Paw Prints (52)

Science Project (82)

Translations (45)

Social Studies – Responsibility

Authors (64)

Breeds (75)

Chores (38)

Commonalities (39)

Debate/Animal Issues (87)

Germs (78)

Grooming (2)

Nurturing (1)

Photo Album (41)

Reminiscing (42)

Sportsmanship (36)

Stressin' (44)

Thanks (37)

Beauty Parlor (31)

Careers (85)

Collage Art (49)

Cultures (86)

Gear Bag (40)

Going For A Walk (55)

Hand Washing (62)

Peanut Butter (58)

Preparing For a Walk (56)

Service Projects (95-101)

Staying Safe (43)

Teaching Tricks (25)

Social Studies – Ethics

Breeds (75)

Commonalities (39)

Debate/Animal Issues (87)

Germs (78)

Chores (38)

Cultures (86)

Family Resemblance (77)

Research (81)

Service Projects (95-101)

Sportsmanship (36)

Staying Safe (43)

Stressin' (44)

Translations (45)

Social Studies – Family

These activities tie in well to lessons about familiar roles.

Chores (38)

Classification (76)

Collage Art (49)

Commonalities (39)

Cultures (86)

Family Resemblance (77)

Follow The Leader (15)

Good Friends (34)

Grooming (2)

Kitchen Time (61)

Head, Shoulders, Knees and Toes (79)

Lights, Camera, Action! (67)

Nurturing (1)

Obstacle Course (20)

Pack Dynamics (88)

Peanut Butter (58)

Photo Album (41)

Reminiscing (42)

Staying Safe (43)

Stressin' (44)

Translations (45)

Social Studies - Health and Safety

Animal Bingo (8)

Careers (85)

Chores (38)

Collage Art (49)

Use this space to add Cognitive/Academic goals of your own.

#6 Petting . . . Callum comforts a client during a therapy session.

Self-Help/ Occupational Goals

See grasping, releasing and fine motor skills for activities that address prerequisites to most of these goals.

Cutting With Scissors

Animal Artists (48)

Collage Art (49)

Knots (97)

Musical Dots (19)

Password (22)

Paw Prints (52)

Shape Up (53)

Tiny Treats (63)

What's Next? (71)

Word Book (72)

Drawing

Animal Artists (48)

Making Copies (50)

Murals (51)

Password (22)

Paw Prints (52)

What's Next? (71)

Dressing

Eating

Handwriting/Pencil Manipulation

Self Care - Personal Hygiene

Beauty Parlor (31)   Candid Camera (32)

Fido Says (13)   Gear Bag (40)

Germs (78)   Grab Bag (14)

Going Visiting *this is a motivator to practice grooming skills* (33)

Grooming (2)   Hand Washing (62)

Lights, Camera, Action! (67)   Word Book (72)

Use this space to add occupational goals of your own.

Speech/Language Goals

Asking and Answering Questions

20 Questions (47)   Animal Genius (94)

Careers (85)   Commonalities (39)

Dance Party (10)   Going Visiting (33)

Grab Bag (14)   Grooming (2)

Photo Album (41)   Picky Eaters (80)

Reminiscing (42)   Research (81)

Science Project (82)   Sit and Share (35)

Special Delivery (93)   Sportsmanship (36)

Step on It (92)   Story Time (70)

Teaching Tricks (25)   Word Book (72)

Word Problems (91)   Zoom In (84)

Clearly Pronouncing Words In a Sentence

Emphasize clearly pronouncing words in spontaneous sentences during any of these activities, through modeling and repetition.

20 Questions (47)   Animal Genius (94)

Expanding Sentences

Some of these activities offer the opportunity to expand the client's spontaneous sentences, other activities are more structured.

Chores (38)

Compare and Contrast (65)

Gear Bag (40)

Good Friends (34)

Grab Bag (14)

Grooming (2)

Nurturing (1)

Photo Album (41)

Reminiscing (42)

Research (81)

Science Project (82)

Silly Sentences (69)

Special Delivery (93)

Step on It (92)

Thanks (37)

The Cup Game (26)

Treat Hunt (28)

What's Next? (71)

Word Book (72)

Word Search (73)

Improving Breath Support/Control

Blowing Bubbles (9)

Grooming (?)

Petting (6) *match breathing to strokes*

Story Time (70)

Yoga (60)

You Blew It! (30)

Increasing Vocabulary

Some interventions offer opportunities for spontaneous teaching of vocabulary, others are more structured.

Adaptations (74)

Animal Bingo (8)

Animal Genius (94)

Beauty Parlor (31)

Candid Camera (32)

Chores (38)

Classification (76)

Going For A Walk (55)

Good Friends (34)

Grab Bag (14)

Grooming (2)

Memory (17)

Head, Shoulders, Knees and Toes (79)

Musical Dots (19)

Nurturing (1)

Password (22)

Photo Album (41)

Picky Eaters (80)

Preparing For a Walk (56)

Research (81)

Scrambled Letters (68)

Silly Sentences (69)

Special Delivery (93)

Step on It (92)

Story Time (70)

The Cup Game (26)

What Now? (29)

Word Book (72)

Word Search (73)

Monitoring Pitch/Phrasing/Volume/Pace

Do any of these activities emphasizing pitch, phrasing, volume and pace.

20 Questions (47)

Authors (64)

Beauty Parlor (31)

Chores (38)

Debate/Animal Issues (87)

Fido Says (13)

Gear Bag (40)

Grooming (2)

Kitchen Time (61)

Nurturing (1)

Photo Album (41)

Reminiscing (42)

Science Project (82)

Sit and Share (35)

Teaching Tricks (25)

The Cup Game (26)

Trivia (46)

Going Visiting (33)

Hide and Seek (16)

Lights, Camera, Action! (67)

Offering Treats (5)

Red Light Green Light (23)

Research (81)

Silly Sentences (69)

Story Time (70)

Thanks (37)

Treat Hunt (28)

Word Search (73)

Producing Specific Phonemes in Beginning/Middle/End of Words

Set up each activity with a specific phoneme and set of words in mind that relate to the activity. For example, using the /t/ sound, you could do the activity "Off and Take It (21)," using the words: take, wait, treat, want, trick, etc.

Animal Genius (94)

Blowing Bubbles (9)

Collage Art (49)

Beauty Parlor (31)

Candid Camera (32)

Counting (90)

Dog-Dog-Cat (11)

Eyes On Me (7)

Fetch (12)

Fido Says (13)

Gear Bag (40)

Grab Bag (14)

Grooming (2)

Hide and Seek (16)

Head, Shoulders, Knees and Toes (79)

Kitchen Time (61)

Memory (17)

Musical Dots (19)

Nurturing (1)

Off and Take It (21)

Offering Treats (5)

Password (22)

Photo Album (41)

Preparing For a Walk (56)

Red Light Green Light (23)

Research (81)

Science Project (82)

Scrambled Letters (68)

Soccer (24)

Special Delivery (93)

Step on It (92)

Teaching Tricks (25)

Thanks (37)

Tiny Treats (63)

Treasure Hunt (27)

Treat Hunt (28)

Trivia (46)

What Now? (29)

Word Book (72)

Word Search (73)

Producing Specific Phonemes When Isolated

Plan each activity with specific phonemes in mind. For example, while washing hands, listening to the sound of the water, have the client work on the /sh/ sound. Activities can also be used as motivation, i.e.: Say /k/ 5 times, and then the animal partner will give you 5.

Animal Genius (94)

Grooming (2)

Hand Washing (62)

Musical Dots (19)

Nurturing (1)

Picky Eaters (80)

Scrambled Letters (68)

Special Delivery (93)

Step on It (92)

Tiny Treats (63)

Word Search (73)

You Blew It! (30)

Strengthening Oral Muscles

Blowing Bubbles (9)

Candid Camera (32) *Take silly pictures making funny faces with the animal, modeled by the professional*

Special Delivery (93)

Step on It (92)

Tongue-ersize (59)

You Blew It! (30)

Using Complete/Coherent Sentences:

These activities allow for spontaneous speech. This provides clients with the opportunity to practice using complete/coherent sentences. This also gives professionals the opportunity to assist the client in reframing and restating incomplete and incoherent sentences.

20 Questions (47)

Beauty Parlor (31)

Chores (38)

Debate/Animal Issues (87)

Gear Bag (40)

Grab Bag (14)

Lights, Camera, Action! (67)

Offering Treats (5)

Picky Eaters (80)

Research (81)

Silly Sentences (69)

Teaching Tricks (25)

The Cup Game (26)

Trivia (46)

Word Book (72)

Word Search (73)

Authors (64)

Candid Camera (32)

Compare and Contrast (65)

Fido Says (13)

Going Visiting (33)

Grooming (2)

Nurturing (1)

Photo Album (41)

Reminiscing (42)

Science Project (82)

Sit and Share (35)

Thanks (37)

Treat Hunt (28)

What's Next? (71)

Word Problems (91)

Use this space to add speech goals of your own.

#96 Yarns. . . A client shows Tate
the sweater she knitted for him.

Appendix A:
Animal Themed Songs

These songs are from all eras, all genres. It's a good idea to listen to the songs before playing them for your clients to make sure the lyrics and message are a good match for your clients and their goals.

Songs Related To Dogs

Atomic Dog - George Clinton

B-I-N-G-O – Traditional Folk Song

Bird Dog - The Everly Brothers

Canis Lupis - the Aquabats

Dinner Bell? - They Might Be Giants

Dixie the Tiny Dog – Peter Himmelman

Dog - The Eddie Adcock Band

Everything Reminds Me of My Dog - Jane Siberry

Gonna Buy Me a Dog - The Monkees

Happy Little Nobody's Waggy Tail Dog – Earl King

Hound Dog - Elvis

How Much Is That Doggie In The Window? Patti Page

I Found My Best Friend In the Dog Pound – Burl Ives

I Love My Dog - Cat Stevens

I Want A Dog - The Pet Shop Boys

Lilly - Pink Martini

Little Brown Dog - Taj Mahal

Me and My Arrow - Harry Nilsson

Me and You and a Dog Named Boo – Lobo

My Dog Loves Your Dog – Ray Henderson

Oh Where, Oh Where Has My Little Dog Gone? Susie Tallman

Old Blue – The Byrds

Opposable Thumb - Dan Bern

Tennessee Hound Dog - Osborne Brothers

The Dog Song - Nellie McKay

The Poodle Dog Song – Jimmie Davis

The Puppy Song - Harry Nilsson

The Terrier Song -Kids in the Hall

Walking The Dog - Rufus Thomas

Who Let the Dogs Out? - Baha Men

Your Adorable Beast - Bobby Bare Jr.

Songs Related To Cats

Everybody Wants to be a Cat – Disney, Aristocats

Phenomenal Cat - The Kinks

Stray Cat Strut – Stray Cats

The Cat Came Back – The Muppets

The Cat In The Window – Petula Clark

The Cat Song - Ray Stevens
Walk Right In – The Rooftop Singers
Walking My Cat Named Dog – Dr. Hook and the Medicine Show

Songs Related To Horses

A Horse With No Name - America
All the Pretty Little Ponies - Kenny Loggins
Appaloosa - Geno Vannelli
Camptown Races - Steven Foster
Eagles and Horses - John Denver
Ghost Riders in the Sky – Johnny Cash
Girls and Horses - Templeton Thompson
Heavy Horses - Jethro Tull
Horses in Heaven - Dan Roberts
I Ride An Old Paint - Michael Martin Murphey
Let 'em Run – Lacy J Dalton
Live Like Horses - Elton John
May The Horse Be With You - Relient K
My Pony Knows the Way - Tom Paxton
Old Faithful - Eddy Arnold
Old Paint - Linda Ronstadt
Old Red - Marty Robbins
Palomino Days - Michael Martin Murphey
Ponies – John Denver
Rhythm of the Hoof Beats - Gene Autry

Run for the Roses - Dan Fogelberg

Silver Palomino – Bruce Springsteen

Tennesee Stud – Jimmy Driftwood

The Chesapeake Bay - Gene Watson

The Chestnut Mare - The Byrds

The Heart of the Appaloosa - Fred Small

The Horses - Rickie Lee Jones

The Horsey Song - Mike Oldfield

The Pony Man - Michael Martin Murphey

The Strawberry Roan - Marty Robbins

Wild Horses - Natasha Bedingfield

Wildfire - Michael Martin Murphey

Songs Related To Birds

A Little Bird Told Me – Evelyn Knight

A Little White Duck - Burl Ives

Beautiful Bluebird – Neil Young

Bird Song – Grateful Dead

Birdhouse in Your Soul – They Might Be Giants

Birdland – Ella Fitzgerald

Birds of a Feather - Phish

Blackbird – The Beatles

Bluebirds in the Moonlight – Glen Miller

Bye Bye Blackbird – Frank Sinatra

Cry of the Wild Goose – Frankie Laine

Feed the Birds – Disney, Mary Poppins

Fly Like An Eagle – The Steve Miller Band

Free as a Bird – Beatles

Hummingbird – Wilco

Kookaburra Sits in the Old Gum Tree – Marion Sinclair

Let's Turkey Trot – Little Eva

Little Bird – Annie Lennox

Little Red Rooster – Rolling Stones

Lullaby of Birdland – Sarah Vaughan

Mockin' Bird Hill – Patti Page

Raven – Jewel

Rockin Robin – Jackson Five

Snowbird – Anne Murray

Songbird – Eva Cassidy

Sparrow in the Treetop - Guy Mitchell

Surfin Bird – The Trashmen

Tennessee Bird Walk – Jack Blanchard & Misty Morgan

The Birds and the Bees – Dean Martin

The Bluebird, the Buzzard, and the Oriole – Bobby Day

The Chicken Dance – Werner Thomas

The Cuckoo's Call – Edgar Selden

Three Little Birds – Bob Marley

Turkey in The Straw –– Dan Bryant

When the Red Red Robin – Bing Crosby

When the Swallows Come Back to Capistrano – Gene Autry

White Bird – It's a Beautiful Day
Woody Woodpecker Song – Kay Kyser
Yellow Bird – Chris Isaak

**Unfortunately, besides *Little Bunny Foo Foo* and songs about the Easter Bunny, songs about small animals seem to be nonexistent.

#3 Up Close and Personal... A client snuggles with Chelsea

Appendix B: Recipes For Animal Treats

Because many animals are picky eaters, have food allergies, or sensitive stomachs, consult with the handler before making and offering any treats.

Dog Treats

Paw Lick'n Chick'n Biscuits

2 c. white flour

¾ c. yellow cornmeal

1/3 c. oatmeal

1 c. shredded carrot

2 crushed chicken bouillon cubes

1 c. chicken broth

4 Tbsp softened margarine

1 egg

1 Tbsp milk

½ t. garlic powder

Heat oven to 325 degrees F.

Combine all ingredients. Knead dough for three minutes. Apply a light layer of flour to rolling surface and pin. Roll dough to ¼-inch thickness and cut into shapes. Beat eggs and milk together and apply to top of biscuits with a brush.

Bake 35 minutes.

Apple Cinnamon Doggie Treats

5 ounces dried apples, finely chopped

1 teaspoon cinnamon

1 tablespoon parsley flakes

1 cup ice water

5 cups flour

1/2 cup plus 1 tablespoon corn oil

1/2 cup carnation powdered milk

2 eggs

Heat oven to 350 degrees F.

Chop the dried apples. A food processor works well for this.

Place the apples, cinnamon, parsley, water, oil, flour, dry milk and eggs in a large bowl and mix well until dough forms. On a lightly floured surface, roll out the dough to ¼-inch thickness. Cut into desired shapes and place on cookie sheets. Bake 20 to 25 minutes.

Chilly Paws Ice Cream

32 ounces vanilla yogurt

1 mashed banana or one large jar of baby fruit or meat

2 tablespoons peanut butter

2 tablespoons honey (optional)

Blend all ingredients together and freeze in paper cups or ice cube trays.

Peanut Butter Carob Chip Cookies

2 cups whole wheat flour

1 tablespoon baking powder

1 cup carob chips

1 cup smooth or chunky peanut butter

1 cup low-fat or whole milk

2 eggs

1/4 cup honey

Heat oven to 375 degrees F.

Combine the flour and baking powder in a large bowl. In a smaller bowl combine the peanut butter, milk, eggs, and honey. Mix well until combined. Add the milk mixture to the dry ingredients and mix with a hand beater. After the ingredients are mixed, add the carob chips, just until combined. Drop the cookies onto an ungreased cookie sheet. Bake for about 20 minutes. Let stand one minute, then remove from cookie sheet. Place on a cookie rack to cool.

Pupsicles

2 cups beef or chicken broth

2/3 cup water

2 or 3 ice cube trays

Small rawhide sticks

Mix water with beef or chicken broth and pour into ice cube trays. Place in freezer. Add a rawhide stick halfway through the freezing. It's probably best to serve this dish outside, as they can be a bit messy.

Cat Treats

Su-purr Kitty Cookies

1 cup whole wheat flour

1 (6 ounce) can tuna in oil, undrained

1 tablespoon vegetable oil or bacon grease

1 egg

Combine all ingredients; mix well; add small amounts of water if mixture is too thick. Turn dough onto a lightly floured surface and roll out to 1/4-inch thick. Cut shapes with a cookie cutter and place 1 inch apart on an ungreased cookie sheet. Bake at 350 degrees F for 20 minutes, or until firm.

Tuna Pops

Liquid left over from tuna packed in spring water

A few pinches of tuna.

Drain the liquid from tuna packed in spring water into mini ice cube trays. Sprinkle the tuna over the top and freeze. Give no more than two cubes at a time as a treat. Reuse your can of drained tuna by placing it in an airtight container and covering with filtered water overnight for a second batch of tuna-pop water.

Kitty Salad

Especially good for cats who eat houseplants!

1 small carrot, peeled and finely grated

1/2 cup chopped sprouts

2 teaspoons finely chopped fresh parsley

1/2 teaspoon fresh catnip

2 tablespoons vegetable broth

Blend carrot, sprouts, parsley and catnip in a medium-size bowl. Add broth and lightly toss. Serve in small portions.

Fish Balls

7-ounces sardines in oil

1/4 cup powdered milk

½ cup wheat germ

Heat oven to 350 degrees.

Mash the sardines along with the oil, and mix in the remaining ingredients. Roll the fish dough into small balls and place them on a greased cookie sheet. Flatten the fish balls with a fork, and bake 10 minutes until they begin to brown.

Catnip Cookies

1/3 cup baking mix

1 egg yolk, beaten

1 tablespoon wheat germ

2/3 cup ground turkey, cooked

1 large egg

2 tablespoons water

1 cup dried catnip,

Heat oven to 350° F.

Grease a cookie sheet with non-stick spray.

Place your cooked turkey meat in a food processor or blender, and blend until it becomes a thick paste. In a large mixing bowl, mix the turkey, wheat germ, ½ cup dried catnip (you'll use the rest later), whole egg, baking mix, and your water. Now roll the mixture into small balls. Roll them in the rest of the dried catnip that you set aside before.

Bake 5 - 8 minutes. They should be soft but firm.

Bird Treats

Squawking Good PB & J

4 slices whole wheat bread

2 t or less peanut butter (creamy or crunchy)

2 t raisins or other sugar-free dried fruit

Using a cookie or biscuit cutter, cut a shape from the center of each slice of bread. Spread a very thin layer of peanut butter on one side of each shape. On two of the shapes, sprinkle a few raisins or chunks of the bird's favorite dried fruit, such as banana chips, apples, or peaches. Top them with the two remaining shapes, and then press around the sides of the sandwiches using your thumb and forefinger, to seal them.

Polly's Popsicles

Fresh Fruits   Nuts (optional)

Birdseed

Blend all ingredients until they form a smooth paste. Pour the mixture into popsicle molds or ice trays. Freeze the pops until they are solid. As an option, you can cover the trays with plastic wrap, and insert halved popsicle sticks through the wrap and into the pops before freezing, to give your bird something to hang on to. Any combination of fruits, nuts and seeds can be used.

Birdie Crackers

Peanut butter   12 saltine crackers
Bird seed

Spread a thin layer of peanut butter on both sides of the crackers and dip in the bird seed, completely covering the cracker. Let sit for about 15 minutes. The cracker will soften a little. Punch a hole in the top and attach a ribbon for hanging.

A Sweet Tweet

4 sliced apples   1 ½ cups shredded carrots

½ cup chopped nuts   ¼ cup raisins

¼ cup dried banana chips   1 tbsp. wheat flour

1 egg (shell optional)   1 tbsp. vegetable oil

1 cup fruit juice   3 tbsp. honey

Preheat oven to 350 degrees.

Arrange the apple slices in the bottom of a 1-quart baking dish. Place the dried banana chips, raisins, carrots, and the nuts on top of the apples and set aside. In a medium sized mixing bowl, combine the egg, vegetable oil, and fruit juice. Pour this mixture over the fruit and nuts. Sprinkle the wheat flour over the top as evenly as possible. Next, drizzle the honey over the entire dish and place it in the oven. Bake the dish for approximately 45 minutes. Let it cool completely, cut and serve. Refrigerate leftovers.

Horse Treats

Horse Cookies

1 cup uncooked oatmeal	1 cup flour
1 cup shredded carrots	1 teaspoon salt
1 tablespoon granulated sugar	2 tablespoons corn oil
¼ cup water	¼ cup molasses

Mix ingredients in a bowl in the order listed. Make small balls and place on a greased cookie sheet. Bake at 350 degrees F for 15 minutes or until golden brown.

Horsey Granola

6 apples, quartered	2 cups Quaker oats
8 carrots, cut in three inch pieces	
1 cup sweet feed	Molasses

Combine all ingredients and fold in enough molasses to make the oats and grain stick to the fruit. Chill overnight and serve.

Carrot, Apple Munchies

1 cup sweet feed	2 cups bran
1 cup flax seed	4 large carrots, shredded
1 cup molasses	½ cup brown sugar
1 cup applesauce	

Mix the dry ingredients. In another bowl, mix molasses, brown sugar, carrots and applesauce. Gradually combine both mixtures. Add only enough molasses mixture to form a thick dough, add more bran if necessary. Using a tablespoon, drop batter onto a foil-lined cookie sheet and flatten slightly. Bake at 300 degrees F for about one hour. Flip and bake for an additional 45 minutes until they are dried out. Keep checking to make sure they don't burn.

Galloping Good Muffins

1 ½ cups bran	1 cup whole wheat flour
1 teaspoon baking soda	1 teaspoon baking powder
¾ cup skimmed milk	½ cup molasses
2 tablespoons corn oil	1 egg, beaten

Stir together bran, flour, soda, and baking powder. Mix together milk, molasses, oil and egg. Mix wet ingredients into dry ingredients. Bake in greased or paper lined muffin tins at 400 degrees F for 15 minutes.

Small Animal Treats

Crunchy Broccoli Treats

A few pieces of broccoli

Honey   Birdseed

Spread a little honey on the broccoli. Sprinkle the birdseed on the honey. Yum!

Cavy Cookies

2 c. whole wheat flour   1 c. shredded carrot

¼ c. shredded apple   1 c. warm water

2 Tbsp honey

Preheat oven to 350 degrees.
Mix the ingredients into a fairly stiff dough. If the mixture is not firm enough, add some more flour. Roll to 1/4 inch thickness on a lightly floured surface and cut into shapes. Bake for 9-12 minutes, until edges are crispy.

Little Critter Salad

1 Tbsp orange juice   ½ c. spinach

1 chopped carrot   a few very juicy strawberries

Mix ingredients together and serve!

Fruit Snacks

A few berries (strawberries work well)

1 peeled and cored apple   1 celery stalk

2/3 c. flour   1/3 c. water

Preheat oven to 350 degrees.

Blend ingredients until a mush is formed-may be chunky or smooth, depending on preference. Drop teaspoon sized spoonfuls onto a baking sheet about 1-inch apart. Bake for 6-10 minutes or until brown. Let them set for about three minutes before removing from the cookie sheet.

Summertime Frosty Cubes

Food pellets

Hot water

Fruit

Mix some food pellets with a little hot water, just enough to soak in and turn them mushy. Spoon the pellet mixture into an ice-cube tray. Put a small piece of fruit on top of each if you want. Freeze the cubes and offer on a hot day!

Appendix C: Animal-Related Children's Literature

This is definitely not a comprehensive list of literature. There are many more fabulous books to be discovered. Consult your local library or the internet for a current, comprehensive list.

Dog-Related Children's Literature

Board Books

Busy Doggies – John Schindel

Dog - Matthew Van Fleet

Doggies – Sandra Boynton

Good Dog Carl – Alexandra Day (*There are several in the series and they are all fabulous*)

Pat Them Gently – Melanie O'Brien

Snuggle Puppy – Sandra Boynton

Spot – Eric Hill (*This is another great series*)

That's Not My Puppy – Its Coat Is Too Hairy – Fiona Watt

Picture Books

Bad Dog Marley- John Grogan (*About loving a dog even though he's trouble*)

Bark George – Jules Fifer

Before You Were Mine – Maribeth Boelts (*addresses adoption*)

Biscuit Goes To School - Alyssa Satin Capucilli (*easy reader*)

Buddy Unchained – Daisy Bix (*Buddy is rescued from a neglectful owner*)

Clifford, The Big Red Dog – Norman Bridwell (*a fun, popular series*)

Dog Breath – Dave Pilkey (*a dog with bad breath ends up saving the day*)

Dog Heaven – Cynthia Rylant (*addresses losing a dog to death*)

Dogku – (*collection of poetry*)

Fancy Nancy and the Posh Puppy – Jane O'Connor (*choosing the right dog for your family*)

Go Dog Go! – P.D. Eastman (*easy reader*)

Help Me Mr. Mutt: Answers For Dogs With People Problems - Janet Stevens, Susan Stevens Crummel

It's Hard to Read a Map With a Beagle on Your Lap – Marilyn Singer (*poetry*)

Katie Loves the Kittens – John Nimmelman (*good friends can be different*)

Martha Walks The Dog - Susan Meddaugh (*Martha solves a bully problem with kindness*)

Murphy and Kate – Ellen Howard (*addresses losing a dog to death*)

My Buddy - David Milgrim

Rugby and Rosie – Nan Parson Rossiter (*A family raises Seeing Eye Dogs*)

Sit Truman – Dan Harper

Some Dog – Mary Casanova (*A dog worries that it's not important anymore*)

Superdog Heart of a Hero - Caralyn and Mark Buehner (*A dog is a hero despite what others say*)

The Old Woman Who Named Things – Cynthia Rylant (*A lonely old woman refuses to get close to anyone she may outlive. Then the dog comes along and works his way into her heart.*)

The Other Dog – Madeline L'Engle (*Welcoming a new baby into the house*)

Walter the Farting Dog – William Kotzwinkle, Glenn Murray (*The smelly dog becomes the hero*)

Chapter Books

Because of Winn Dixie – Kate DiCamillo

Henry and Mudge – Cynthia Rylant

Ol' Yeller – Fred Gipson (*sad ending*)

Shiloh – Phyllis Reynolds Naylor

Sounder – William Howard Armstrong (*sad ending*)

Stone Fox – John Reynolds Gardiner

The Captain's Dog – Roland Smith (*Lewis and Clark through the eyes of a dog*)

The Dog Who Wouldn't Be – Farley Mowat

Tornado – Betsy Byars

Where the Red Fern Grows – Wilson Rawls *(sad ending)*

Nonfiction

A Dog's Gotta Do What a Dog's Gotta Do – Marilyn Singer
    (working dogs and their jobs)

Are You Ready For Me? - Claire Buchwald *(how to prepare for a
    dog)*

Complete Dog Book For Kids – American Kennel Club

Dog Eyewitness Books – Julie Clutton Brock

The First Dog – Jan Brett

Cat Related Children's Literature

Board Books

Cat – Matthew Van Fleet

Have You Seen My Cat? – Eric Carle

That's Not My Kitten – Fiona Watt and Rachel Wells

Picture Books

Bad Kitty – Nick Bruel

Cat Heaven – Cynthia Rylant (*where cats go when they die*)

Charlie Anderson – Barbara Ambercrombie (*this cat has two houses and two families, like many children*)

Cookie's Week – Cindy Ward

For the Love of Autumn – Patricia Polocco

Kitten's First Full Moon – Kevin Henkes

Millions of Cats – Wanda Gag (*humility vs. vanity*)

Mr. Putter and Tabby – Cynthia Rylant and Arthur Howard (*a fun series*)

Skippy Jon Jones - Judy Schachner

Splat The Cat – Rob Scotton (*about friendship and the first day of school*)

The Cat In The Hat – Dr. Seuss

The Gift of Nothing – Patrick McDonnell (*about friendship*)

The Pigeon Books – Mo Willems

The Tenth Good Thing About Barney – Judith Viorst (*about the death of a pet cat*)

Wabi Sabi – Mark Reibstein

Chapter Books

Meow Means Mischief – Ann Nagda

Miranda the Great – Elenor Estes

Pioneer Cat – William H Hooks

Socks – Beverly Cleary (*Socks gets a new baby in the house*)

The Dancing Cats of Applesap – Janet Taylor Lisle

The Klondike Cat – Julie Lawson

The Storm – Cynthia Rylant

The Stranger Next Door – Peg Kehret

Warriors: The New Prophesy – Erin Hunter

Whittington – Alan Armstrong (*about dyslexia*)

Nonfiction

Cats to The Rescue: True Tales of Heroic Felines – Marilyn Singer and Jean Cassels

Encyclopedia of Cat Breeds – Anne Helgren

How to Talk To Your Cat – Jean Craighead George & Paul Meisel

The Ultimate Encyclopedia of Cats, Cat Breeds and Cat Care – Alan
  Edwards

Totally Fun Things To Do With Your Cat – Maxine Rock

Why Do Cats Meow? – Joan Holub

Horse Related Children's Literature

Board Books

Little Ponies – Christina Gunzi

That's Not My Pony – Fiona Watt and Rachel Wells

Touch and Feel Ponies – DK Publishing

Picture Books

Big Red – Walter Farley

Billy and Blaze: A Boy and His Horse – CW Anderson

Black Cowboy: Wild Horses – Julius Lester

Bronco Busters – Alison Herzig (*kindness pays*)

Fritz and the Beautiful Horses – Jan Brett

Horsefly – Alice Hoffman (*conquering fear*)

Little Black – Walter Farley (*friendship*)

Magical Mac –Michelle S Davis & Alexandra Makris

Mrs. Mack – Patricia Polocco

My Pony – Susan Jeffers

Mystic Horse – Paul Goble

On the Trail With Miss Pace – Sharon P Denslow

The Horse in Harry's Room – Sid Hoff

The Thunderherd – Kathi Applet

Chapter Books

Beware The Mare – Jessie Haas

Black Stallion Series – Walter Farley

Heartland Series – Lauren Brooke

Little Horse – Betsy Byars

More Than a Horse – C.S. Adler

National Velvet – Enid Bagnold

Pony Pals Series – Jean Betancourt

Riding Freedom – Pam Munoz Ryan

Saddle Club Series – Bonnie Bryant

Touch the Moon – Marion Dane Bauer

Nonfiction

DK Horse and Pony Book – Carolyn Henderson

Horse Crazy – Jessie Haas

Horses! – Gail Gibbons

My First Horse and Pony Book Draper and Matthew Roberts

Why Do Horses Neigh? - Joan Holub and Anna DiVito

Small Animal–Related Children's Literature

Board Books

If You Were My Bunny - Kate Mcmullan and David Mcphail

Pat the Bunny (Touch and Feel Book) - Dorothy Kunhardt

Picture Books

Brian & Bob: The Tale of Two Guinea Pigs - Georgie Ripper

Charlie Hits It Big - Deborah Blumenthal and Denise Brunkus

Emmaline and the Bunny - Katherine Hannigan

Goodnight Moon - Margaret Wise Brown and Clement Hurd

Guinea Pigs Don't Read Books (A Puffin Unicorn) - Colleen
    Stanley Bare

Howard B. Wigglebottom Learns About Bullies - Howard Binkow
    and Susan F. Cornelison

Howard B. Wigglebottom Learns to Listen - Howard Binkow and
    Susan F. Cornelison

I Love Guinea-pigs - Dick King-Smith and Anita Jeram

It's Not Easy Being a Bunny - Marilyn Sadler

Jeremy: The Tale of an Honest Bunny - Jan Karon and Teri Weidner

Marshmallow - Clare Turlay Newberry

Max and Ruby's Busy Week - Rosemary Wells (*a complete series*)

One Guinea Pig Is Not Enough - Kate Duke

Super Guinea Pig to the Rescue - Udo Weigelt and Nina Spranger

The Runaway Bunny - Margaret Wise Brown and Clement Hurd

White Rabbit's Color Book - Alan Baker

Chapter Books

Fluffy Goes To School - Kate Mcmullan and Mavis Smith

Guinea Pig in the Garage - Ben M. Baglio, Jenny Gregory, and Shelagh McNicholas

Jenius: The Amazing Guinea Pig - Dick King-Smith and Brian Floca

Nonfiction

A Rabbit for You: Caring for Your Rabbit - Blackaby, Susan, Delage, and Charlene

Guinea Pigs - Mark Evans, Laura S. Jeffrey

My Guinea Pig and Me - Immanuel Birmelin

Rabbit (ASPCA Pet Care Guides) - Mark Evans

Taking Care of your Rabbit Book - Barrons Books

More Resources

For more information on animal-assisted therapy, here are some resources with which to start.

Websites

Delta Society: http://www.deltasociety.org
Dogplay: http://dogplay.com/Activities/Therapy/index. html#overview
Therapy Dogs Incorporated: http://www.therapydogs.com/
Therapy Dogs International: http://www.tdi-dog.org/

Books

Animal-Assisted Therapy: Therapeutic Interventions by The Delta Society
Handbook On Animal-Assisted Therapy by Aubrey H. Fine (Editor)
Therapy Dogs Today - Their Gifts, Our Obligation by Kris Butler
Therapy Dogs: Compassionate Modalities Book & DVD by Kris Butler

For teaching dogs to do tricks:

101 Dog Tricks: Step by Step Activities to Engage, Challenge, and Bond with Your Dog by Kyra Sundance and Chalcy

Dog Tricks: Step by Step by Mary Ann Rombold Zeigenfuse and Jan Walker

Silly Dog Tricks: Fun for You and Your Best Friend by D. Caroline Coile

Take a Bow Wow: Virginia Broitman/ North Star Canines & Company (A dvd that shows positive clicker trick training)

The Only Dog Tricks Book You'll Ever Need: Impress Friends, Family--and Other Dogs! by Gerilyn J. Bielakiewicz and Paul S. Bielakiewicz

About the Author

Stacy Grover is a Delta Society Pet Partner, Evaluator, and Instructor, and is a member of Therapy Animals of Utah. She has participated in animal-assisted therapy with animal partners Cosita and Liberty in various rehab, hospice, and skilled nursing facilities, a lockdown facility for teens, a drug rehab center, and a children's hospital. If she's not teaching her class of fourth graders or volunteering, you might find her up on the side of a mountain, hiking with Cosita and Liberty.

Photo taken by Shay Voorhees, photographybyshay.com